Young Reed

Encyclopedia of World Animals

First published in Australia in 2008 by Young Reed
An imprint of New Holland Publishers (Australia) Pty Ltd
Sydney • Auckland • London • Cape Town

1/66 Gibbes Street Chatswood NSW 2067 Australia
218 Lake Road Northcote Auckland New Zealand
86 Edgware Road London W2 2EA United Kingdom
80 McKenzie Street Cape Town 8001 South Africa

10 9 8 7 6 5 4 3 2 1

National Library of Australia Cataloguing-in-Publication Data:
Rohr, Ian.

Young reed encyclopedia of world animals / Ian Rohr.
ISBN: 9781921580253 (pbk.)
Includes index.
For primary age children.
Animals—Encyclopedias, Juvenile.
591.03

Publisher: Fiona Schultz
Publishing Manager: Lliane Clarke
Project Editor: Jenny Scepanovic
Editor: Shelley Barons
Designers: Tiffany Faulder, Tania Gomes
Production Manager: Linda Bottari
Printed in Singapore by Tien Wah Press

Picture credits
Getty Images
6, 8, 9, 10, 11, 12b, 13, 14t, 15, 16, 17, 18, 19, 20, 21, 22, 23t, 25, 26, 27, 28, 29b, 30, 31, 32, 33, 34, 35, 37, 38, 39, 41t, 43, 44, 45b, 48, 49, 52, 53t, 54, 55, 56, 57, 58, 59, 60, 61, 63b, 64, 65, 66, 67, 75, 76, 77t, 78, 79, 97b, 108, 109, 112t, 116, 117, 120

Lochman Transparencies
12t, 14b, 24, 36, 45t, 46, 47, 50, 51, 53b, 62, 63t, 69, 70, 71, 72, 73t, 74, 77b, 80, 84, 85, 87, 88, 89t, 90, 91, 93t, 94, 95, 96, 97t, 98, 99, 100, 102, 103, 104, 105, 106, 107, 110, 111, 112b, 113, 114, 115, 118, 119, 121

NHIL
7, 23b, 29t, 40, 41b, 42, 68, 73b, 78, 81, 86, 89b, 92, 93b, 101

Young Reed

Encyclopedia of World Animals

Ian Rohr

young
reed

Contents

Kingdoms, Classes and Species

You might not know what a *Panthera leo* is, but chances are you're familiar with the African lion. If you happen to have a dog you are responsible for a *Canis lupus familiaris*, a domesticated subspecies of the wolf, while *Carassius auratus* often swim around tanks, bowls or ponds and are better known as goldfish.

Classes of their own

Scientists compare the similarities between different animals and then put them into categories based on the results. As part of the examination everything about the animal is looked at. Creatures are studied in the wild, in captivity or under a microscope. Scientists do this so that they, and we, can better understand the animal kingdom.

All animals are part of the kingdom of Animalia; Kingdom is the broadest group. Species and subspecies are the narrowest groups and contain only very closely related animals.

There are five other main categories from species until you get up to kingdom, starting with genus, then family, order, class and phylum. The closer to kingdom you get, the more animals are found in each group. Genus covers creatures that are still close relatives such as the members of the Panthera genus— the lion, leopard, jaguar and tiger. These four are part of the Felidae family along with all other cats. Cats, along with other families such as the Canidae (dog) and Ursidae (bear), are grouped together into the Carnivore order. Cats also come under the class of Mammals and then the phylum of Chordata or vertebrates, animals with bones. This phylum contains many different species, but millions more along with untold individuals enter the picture when the boneless invertebrates are added.

Scientists also use special terms to describe the habits and behaviour of different animals. 'Terrestrial' means something that lives on the land, 'arboreal' refers to a creature that spends most of its time in the trees and 'aerial' is anything that spends a lot of time flying. Water dwellers are known as 'aquatic', or 'semi aquatic' if they spend some time on land, while animals that live in the oceans are known as 'marine'.

Leopard (*Panthera pardus*)

The name game

Animals can have many different names in many different places and languages. To avoid confusion, all animals and plants are given a scientific name made up of two or three parts. These names are the same across the world and are usually written in Latin. The first part of the name is the animal's genus while the second is its species. If there is a third name it refers to a subspecies. By using this method all scientists know that *Panthera leo* refers to lions and *Panthera pardus* to leopards.

An ancient language for modern times

Latin was the language of the Roman Empire and it is still widely used in law and medicine as well as biology.

Australian Sea Lion *(Neophoca cinerea)*

Amphibians

Amphibians were the first vertebrates to move onto dry land, around 360 million years ago. Many of the 5000 plus amphibian species still enjoy the best of both worlds, spending their growing period in the water and their adult lives on land. When on land these cold-blooded, clawless and scale-less creatures are usually found in damp places to prevent their thin moist skins from drying out. There are three orders of amphibians—the wormlike caecilians, the salamanders and newts, and the tailless frogs and toads.

The slender, slippery salamander

Salamanders are long slim amphibians—all have tails and most of the 500 species have four short legs. Most are small creatures, though the giant salamanders of Japan and China can grow to well over a metre (3 feet) in length. And whether big or small, salamanders are secretive and while not rare, are rarely seen. All salamanders are carnivores and are usually terrestrial, but always live in moist habitats such as swamps.

Fire Salamander

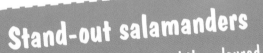

Stand-out salamanders

Many salamanders are brightly coloured and boldly patterned. This is to let predators know that they do not taste good.

Striking salamanders

Salamanders are mostly silent, but some species have a striking way of making their presence known. Using a bone in their throat to build up pressure, salamanders then release their long, sticky, prey-grabbing tongues in a swift shooting motion. With tongues that can extend up to half the length of the salamander's body, there may be no such thing as keeping a safe distance when a salamander is on the hunt!

Caecilian

The nocturnal newts

Newts have drier and rougher skin than their close salamander relatives, but many are also water lovers. As with salamanders, newt habitats can vary—some species are totally aquatic, others divide their time between land and water, while others live their adult lives on land, sometimes in trees. Many are nocturnal, sheltering in rotting logs and under leaf litter by day and emerging at night to feed on insects and other amphibians.

Mysterious caecilians

Not a lot is known about the habits of the earthworm-like caecilians, despite there being nearly 150 different species. This is because legless, small-eyed caecilians spend much of their time underground, using their large, strong skulls to burrow down deep. Most young caecilians are born in the water and head for dry land when they reach maturity. They feed mainly on worms, termites and other insects and can range in size from about 6 centimetres (2 inches) to 1.5 metres (4.5 feet).

Antelopes

Antelopes are a type of two-toed mammal from the ungulate group. Related to sheep, cattle and goats, antelopes are herbivores found throughout Africa, Europe and Asia. There are about 90 species, ranging in size from the enormous eland to the tiny Royal Antelope, standing about 25 centimetres (10 inches) high and weighing just over 1.5 kilograms (3 pounds). All male antelopes have horns and in some species so do the females. Males mostly use their horns to battle other males and occasionally for self-defence against predators.

Where's the water?

You won't often see a waterbuck swimming, but you won't ever see one far from the water's edge either. This is because waterbuck will dive in at the first sign of danger and swim to safety, though they prefer to stay on dry land whenever possible. Waterbucks secrete a smelly and oily substance from their sweat glands, which helps to keep their shaggy fur dry whenever they are in the water.

Good gnus

Wildebeests are large antelopes that are also known as gnus. Both wildebeest species, the black and the blue, live in Africa, where they share the plains with other grass eaters, and predators. During their annual migration, wildebeests must cross rivers where crocodiles lie waiting, which can be bad news for the gnus. Barring an encounter with a crocodile, lion or hyena pack, most wildebeest live to about 15–20 years of age.

Waterbuck

Safety in numbers

Many ungulate species, especially those that dwell on open plains, live in herds. This can have a number of benefits but the main advantage is the safety it provides. The more pairs of eyes and ears there are, the more chance herd animals have of spotting danger before the danger sneaks up on them. Most antelopes are faster than the predators that hunt them, so as long as they have a bit of warning they can usually sprint to safety.

The biggest of the bunch

The eland is the world's largest antelope and the Giant Eland is the larger of the two species, reaching nearly two metres at the shoulder and weighing over 700 kilograms (1500 pounds). Both sexes have long spiralled horns that grow up to a metre in length. These big browsers are found in open woodlands and savannah plains, where they feed on grass and leaves. Finding safety in numbers, they live in herds of up to twenty or more.

The useful eland

The ox-like eland can be domesticated and used for meat, milk, their hides and, being big and strong, as work animals.

Giant Eland

Arachnids

Spiders and scorpions are arachnids—types of arthropods with bodies made up of two segments and eight jointed legs. Mites and ticks are also arachnids, but have one rounded body. Most of the 80,000 arachnid species are solitary terrestrial predators, though there are a few aquatic mite and spider species. Most arachnids are nocturnal and have simple eyes, so sensitive hairs on their legs and bodies help them navigate, find prey and avoid danger.

Bush Tick

Microscopic mites and clinging ticks

All ticks and some mites are parasites. Mites are tiny and rarely noticed and though many live on land or in water, some species are parasites that burrow under the skin or cling to hair and fur. Plants and most animal species, including insects and humans, can be targeted by specialist parasite mites. Ticks are also skin burrowers and capable of spreading a range of dangerous diseases, while mites can produce allergic reactions.

Striking scorpions

Scorpions are found mainly in warm areas. Unlike egg-laying arachnids, scorpions give birth to live young. The newly hatched youngsters crawl up onto the mother's back and cling on for up to two weeks. Once their stings develop and they are able to hunt they strike out on their own. But they had better not wait too long before leaving home—if they overstay their welcome their mother will most likely eat them.

Scorpion

A frog caught in the web of a giant spider.

Arachnids eating

Because they are not able to swallow solids, most arachnids squirt enzymes into their prey that turn the captured creature into an invertebrate slushy, which the arachnid can then suck up! But before they can liquefy their prey they have to catch it. Some spider species build strong and complex webs, others pounce on their prey. Scorpions grab with pincers then inject immobilising venom, while ticks are parasites that burrow into their hosts' skin to feed on their blood.

What makes a web?

All spiders can produce silk, but not all species use it to build webs. Silk can also be produced for wrapping up prey or cocooning eggs and even, for some young spiders, as a balloon-like form of transport. Some spiders are able to produce as many as eight different types of silk, but the best known use of spider silk is for building a wide variety of extremely strong, very flexible prey-trapping webs.

Gigantic Goliath
The world's biggest spider, the Goliath bird-eating spider, is roughly the same size as a dinner plate and weighs over 120 grams (4 oz).

B Bats

Bats are the only mammals capable of true flight. Flapping their wings, which are modified hands and fingers that support a strong membrane, bats can travel great distances—some of the nearly 1000 bat species migrate thousands of kilometres (miles). Flight has helped bats colonise much of the globe and they can be found in all environments except for cold polar regions. About 70 per cent of bats live off night-flying insects, while most other species rely on fruit and flowers for their food.

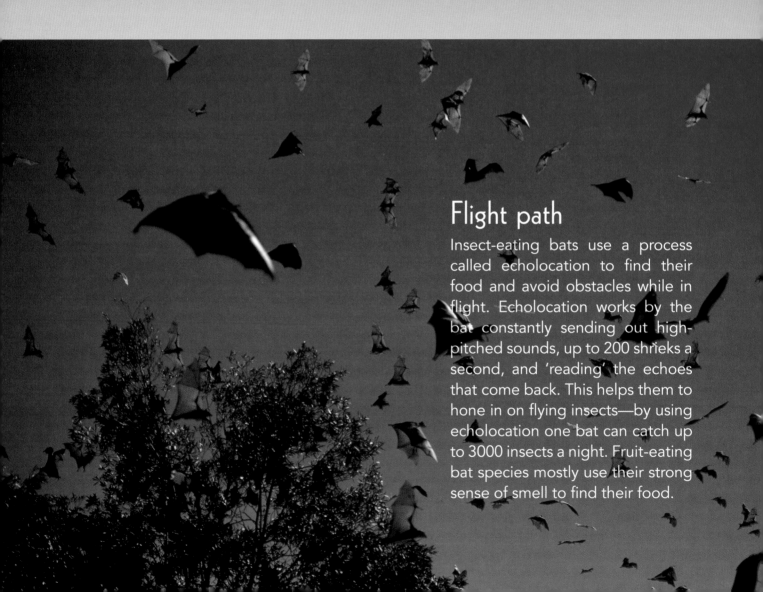

Flight path

Insect-eating bats use a process called echolocation to find their food and avoid obstacles while in flight. Echolocation works by the bat constantly sending out high-pitched sounds, up to 200 shrieks a second, and 'reading' the echoes that come back. This helps them to hone in on flying insects—by using echolocation one bat can catch up to 3000 insects a night. Fruit-eating bat species mostly use their strong sense of smell to find their food.

Bats exiting a cave

Nature's pest controllers

Just one small bat colony can eat over 600 million insects in a year. When it comes to pest control we have a lot to thank bats for.

Caves and colonies

Many of the insect-eating bat species make their home in caves or similar sheltered environments. Different caves, and different parts of caves, are often used for different reasons—to hibernate, to breed, or as a colony for raising young. Even in very large colonies female bats can use the odour and cries of their young to locate them amongst hundreds, thousands or even millions of individuals.

Just hanging around

Most bat species spend their days hanging upside down as they roost in trees, caves or human-built structures such as under bridges or in abandoned buildings and mines. This position allows bats to make a fast take-off if danger threatens or when it is time to go forth and feed. During these dormant daylight hours, the body temperature of many bat species drops to help them conserve energy.

Bats in miniature

At just 30–40 mm (1–1.5 inches) in length and weighing only two grams, the Bumblebee Bat may be the smallest mammal on the planet.

Lapping it up

The three species of vampire bats are found in Central and South America. Vampire bats feed at night, using sharp incisor teeth to cut into the flesh of sleeping animals and lapping up the blood that trickles out. Vampire bat saliva contains ingredients that keep the blood from clotting so that the food keeps flowing. The amount of blood a vampire takes is not enough to cause real harm, but the rabies virus that many carry can be a killer.

Bears

These carnivores are found across the Northern Hemisphere with only one of the eight species living down south—South America's Spectacled Bear. Despite a reputation as fearsome hunters, most bears are omnivorous—only the polar bear lives almost exclusively on meat. All bears have long fur and short tails, sharp claws for digging or slicing and a sense of smell up to seven times stronger than that of humans. This gives bears a nose for sniffing out danger and whatever food might be in the neighbourhood.

Bears in the branches

Sloth bears are mostly nocturnal creatures, feeding and roaming by night and resting during the day. Found in the forests of South-East Asia, sloth bears are excellent climbers and will spend hours just hanging in the trees, like the sloths they are named after. Unlike most bears, they enjoy the company of their fellow bears, and are also fond of termites and honey—the insects are dug out of their mounds and the sticky liquid is raided from beehives.

Giant Panda

A bellyful of bamboo

With its black and white fur, the Giant Panda is one of the world's most recognisable, best loved and increasingly threatened animals. Restricted to the isolated mountains of western China the giant panda needs to eat nearly half of its body weight in bamboo each and every day. As their bamboo forest habitat shrinks, the 1000 or so giant pandas left in the wild are in ever increasing danger of disappearing altogether.

Long-distance swimmers

Polar bears are excellent swimmers and have been spotted up to 100 kilometres (62 miles) from land. Thick layers of fat and long fur keep them warm in the icy waters.

The big brown bears

Like most big carnivores brown bears have been driven into ever shrinking pockets of land. But where there is room to move, brown bears can really get around. Home ranges can extend to 2500 square kilometres (965 square miles), depending on the available food—in plentiful environments the range may be as small as 30–50 square kilometres (11–19 square miles). Finding food occupies a lot of a brown bear's energy, as fat reserves need to be built up to get through the lean winter months.

Kodiak Bear

Polar Bear

Polar bears are large marine mammals found in the harsh environment of the Arctic. Regular travellers, they roam up to 80 kilometres (50 miles) across the ice each day in search of seals and other prey. These patient pursuers will wait for hours by a breathing hole until a seal comes up for air. If the seal isn't swift enough to avoid the swiping paws and claws of the planet's biggest terrestrial carnivore, that breath could well be its last.

Polar Bear and cub

Bees

Close relatives of the wasps and ants, bees are flying insects found on all continents except Antarctica. There are just under 20,000 known species of bees, ranging in size from the 2 millimetre (0.08 inch) dwarf bee to one Indonesian species where the females reach nearly 40 millimetres (1.6 inch) in length. The most familiar bee species is the Western honey bee, long known and kept for its honey-making abilities.

Pollinating power

Flowers are important to bees and so are bees to flowers. Flowering plants attract insects such as bees with interesting petals, perfume and by producing sweet nectar. When a bee feeds from a flower much pollen sticks to its body and when the bee flies on to the next flower some of this pollen falls off. This is known as pollination and it is what allows the plant to make seeds. A relationship such as this where both organisms benefit is known as symbiosis.

Bee teatime

Bees eat pollen and nectar, which is collected by worker bees. Nectar is a sugary liquid which, when the water evaporates, produces honey. Honey is stored in a hive to be used as a food source during the winter months when few plants are flowering. Nectar is collected by a long proboscis, while pollen, a powdery substance, is picked up on the tiny hairs that cover the bee's body, or placed in pollen baskets formed by longer hairs near the hind legs.

Bee feeding on flower

Honeycomb

On the B-list

Many bee species live in large colonies where individuals have specific roles to play. A colony is headed by the queen bee, who can lay up to 1500 eggs a day. Some of these eggs develop into female worker bees while others become drones whose only function is to mate with the queen. Worker bees cannot reproduce and in their two-week lifespan they spend their time obtaining food for the larvae and the queen.

Collapsing colonies

Humans have long kept bees for the honey they produce. But in recent years a strange phenomenon has had beekeepers and scientists scratching their heads. Known as Colony Collapse Disorder, it involves all the worker bees from a colony suddenly disappearing. The cause of these collapses is not yet known, but it could involve pesticides, parasites such as mites, diseases, malnutrition or even radiation from cellular phones.

Her royal bee-ness

When a queen bee leaves an old hive to start a new one she doesn't travel alone—up to 70,000 worker bees go with her, all following in the wing beats of scouts who have found a suitable hive location.

Beetles

There are a lot of animals in the world and a lot of them are beetles —about one in four of all the species on the planet is some type of beetle, with nearly 400,000 species identified so far. Not only are beetles the most numerous of the insects, they can be found in nearly all of Earth's environments. Beetles are separated from other insects by their hard curved forewings, or elytra, which protect the much more delicate hind wings that allow beetles to fly.

Some help and some harm

With so many beetle species it is not surprising that while some can be harmful to human life, others can be very helpful. With most beetles this usually comes down to what they eat. Death Watch Beetles eat old timbers while Potato Beetles feast on potato plants. These species can harm our houses and crops. But many ground beetle species feed on other damaging insects, making them very beneficial beetles.

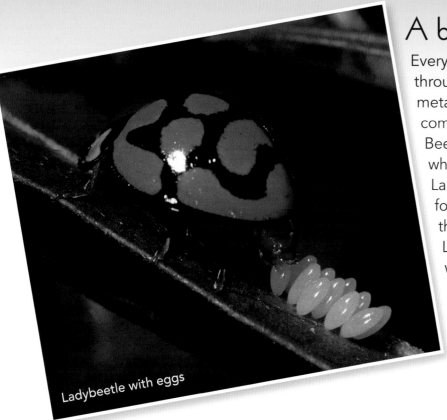

Ladybeetle with eggs

A beetle's life

Every beetle reaches adulthood through a process known as complete metamorphosis. This means that it completely changes its shape. Beetles commence life as eggs, which then hatch into larvae. Larvae look nothing like the adult form, but are able to feed themselves and move around. Larvae then enter a pupa stage where, usually protected by a hard cocoon, they change shape into adult form, emerge from the cocoon and harden.

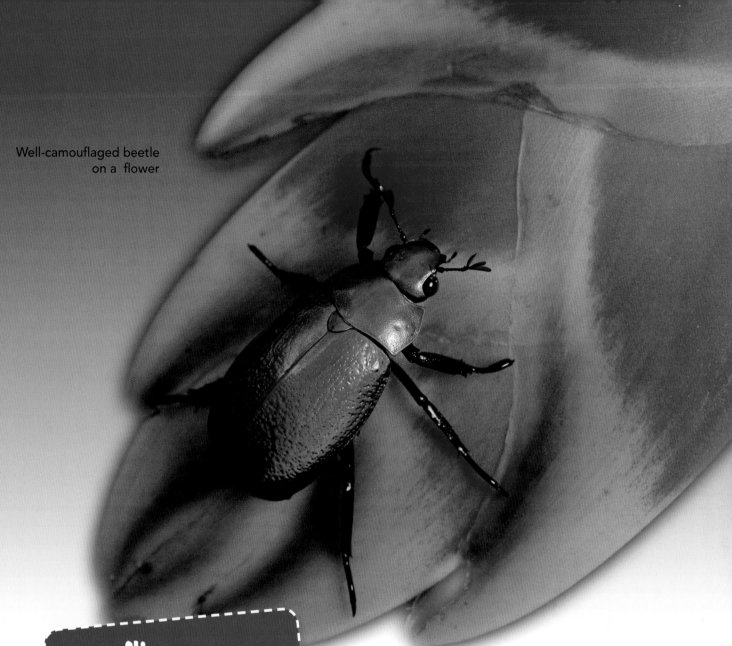

Well-camouflaged beetle on a flower

Not on the menu

It's a tough life for a beetle when so many other creatures see them as a snack. To avoid predators, beetles have built up an impressive range of defence mechanisms. One of these is camouflage, which can make the beetle very difficult to spot. Others use mimicry, which is the ability to not look like a beetle— some species look like wasps, making predators reluctant to approach. The ability to secrete toxic substances is yet another method used by some beetle species to stay safe.

Birds

There are nearly 10,000 species of bird, from the big, earthbound ostrich to the tiny, frantically fluttering hummingbird. Birds evolved from dinosaurs around 150 million years ago and are now found in all of the world's environments. Some birds are home bodies while others are famous for long migrations. Many different bird species can share the same habitat, from seed and insect eaters to flesh-tearing birds of prey. With their dazzling range of plumage, singing abilities and the power of flight, birds have fascinated humans for centuries.

The nesting instinct

All birds lay eggs, though not all species bother to build a nest in which to house them. Bird species that do build nests use a wide variety of materials and construction methods to make shelters for their offspring. Mounds, cups and platforms are all forms of nests built by birds; while sticks, mud, grass and leaves, bark, seaweed, fur and wool are all materials that can be used in nest building.

Chickens rule the world

There are more chickens in the world than there are humans!

Fabulous feathers

Feathers put birds in a class of their own. Their shape and arrangement are crucial for flight control and they help keep birds dry, warm and well camouflaged. When it comes time to put on a show, the brilliant and beautiful patterns found on the feathers of many species provide a stunning display. The number of feathers on a bird can vary enormously, with waterbirds such as swans having up to 25,000.

The peacock's fabulous feathers

Nightingale singing

Singing their song

Birds are the most vocal of creatures, with many species being able to make a wide range of calls or 'sing' a variety of songs. Bird songs are usually made by males to attract females and warn other males away from their territory. Squawking calls can act as an alarm that predators are about, or keep the members of a flock in contact while they are feeding or flying.

Fantastic flight

The ability to fly allows birds to travel more widely than any other animals. Birds fly for many reasons—to find food or a warmer climate, to avoid danger or to search for a mate. Flying can also be a form of communication, such as when birds flutter just above the ground to signal danger down below. And, when you watch some birds going through their moves, it is not hard to imagine that they must also get pleasure from their aerial abilities.

Birds of Prey

Birds of prey are known as raptors, a group that includes over 300 species of eagles, hawks, kites, kestrels, falcons, buzzards and vultures. All raptors are meat-eaters with sharp claws, known as talons, which are used for grasping their prey, and hooked beaks that are used to then tear the prey to pieces. Raptors can range in size from huge condors to the sparrow-sized falconets of South-East Asia, but all have keen eyesight and are expertly adapted for hunting their preferred prey.

The plummeting Peregrine

When it comes to speed, the Peregrine Falcon is the one to beat—not only is it the fastest raptor and fastest bird, it is the fastest creature on the planet. Peregrine Falcons have a cruising speed of up to 90 kilometres (56 miles) an hour, but it is when they are swooping down onto prey that they really make the record books. Figures vary wildly, but a diving speed of at least 300 kilometres (185 miles) an hour is typical for this rapid raptor.

Awesome eagles

Eagles, such as Australia's Wedge-tail, can spot rabbits and other small prey from over 1.5 kilometres (1640 yards) away. This keen eyesight, along with large and powerful bodies, makes eagles very efficient predators. Eagles are among the largest and heaviest birds of prey and inhabit a wide range of habitats. Like many raptors, eagles form breeding pairs that mate for life and cooperate in catching food for the ever-hungry chicks.

Wedgetail eagle

Snail cruncher

The South American Snail Kite is a fussy eater with a taste for crustaceans—it feeds exclusively on the water snails found in its marshy home.

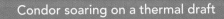

Floating on thermals

Many birds, not just raptors, take advantage of thermal currents to keep flying without using up all the energy that constant flapping requires. Thermal currents are pockets of rising air and birds can use these when they are migrating or, in the case of raptors, soaring high above the ground searching for prey. Thermals allow birds such as eagles and vultures to stay aloft for many hours without tiring themselves out.

An American Bald Eagle feeds its young

Sibling rivalry

Raptors generally have no more than three chicks, but even three is too many to be comfortably feed when times get tough. Rather than waiting for the parents to play favourite, the largest, strongest chick will push its weaker brothers or sisters from the nest, peck them to death, or just make sure they get most of the food the parents bring back, condemning their siblings to a slow death by starvation. In times of plenty, however, all the chicks will be successfully raised.

25

Bison

Bison are nomadic grazing mammals, related to cattle and buffalo. There are two species—the American and the European bison. Bison are big beasts, reaching 2 metres tall, 3 metres in length and weighing up to 900 kilograms. Shaggy-coated creatures, bison come equipped with short, curved horns used for self-defence and the occasional in-herd power struggle. Because of their size and the protection of the herd, bison have few natural predators except when young, old or sick.

A walking general store

The Native Americans who lived on the prairies relied on the bison for many necessities. Beyond the large amounts of meat provided by a bison, its fur and skin were made into blankets, clothes and leather. Bones were fashioned into tools and weapons, while the fat was used as grease and the sinews dried for bow strings. Even the feet and droppings had their uses—glue was made from boiled hooves and dried dung was a fuel for fires.

Stampeding bison herd

Slaughter on the prairie

Bison were easy game when Europeans first moved onto the prairies in the nineteenth century. Such was the slaughter that the bison was almost driven to extinction. They were killed mainly for their skins—once the skin was removed the carcass was often left to rot. Professional hunters could kill hundreds of buffalo a day and thousands in a lifetime. This reduced the population from an estimated 60 million in 1800 to fewer than 600 individuals by the late 1800s.

Europe's biggest land mammal

The slightly smaller European Bison was also almost hunted to extinction and now only survives in fragments of eastern European forests. Once widespread from Britain to Siberia, by the 1920s the last wild bison had been shot and only about 50 survived in zoos. Forest dwellers, unlike their grassland living American relatives, there are now about 2000 reintroduced European Bison living the wild life.

European Bison

Bison or Wisent?
Another name for the European Bison is the Wisent.

The bison bounces back

Fortunately for the bison, some people did not want to see the great herds wiped out. A few individuals set up breeding herds, using the remaining animals to begin rebuilding the bison population. Through the efforts of these people, and a growing awareness on the part of the public and governments, bison are now out of danger. There are currently around 350,000 bison in the USA, many of them in protected reserves and national parks.

Burrowing Animals

Burrow builders tend to be smaller animals—the insectivores and small carnivores that run a high risk of ending up as dinner for something bigger whenever they are out and about. Burrows provide a safer place to eat, sleep and raise young. A burrow doesn't guarantee safety—some predators slither in or dig the burrowers out—but it is certainly safer than out in the open, where many pairs of eyes can be watching and waiting.

Going underground

Burrowing animals share many adaptations that help them lead a subterranean life, including strong claws and forelimbs for digging. Some animals have specific adaptations, such as the wombat's pouch facing backwards, preventing it from filling up with dirt. Generally, the more time an animal spends underground the more specialised adaptations it will have. Moles spend nearly their entire lives digging underground and have tiny eyes, very big forelimbs, sensitive muzzles and spade-like claws.

Moles in holes

Moles live in extensive underground residences, complete with separate areas for resting, nesting and food finding. Young are raised in chambers lined with leaves while foraging tunnels are dug to catch worms, slugs and other small creatures that fall into the space. A mole can dig up to 20 metres (65 feet)of tunnel in a day and the networks can reach a total length of 200 metres (650 feet). Often the only sign of all this underground activity is small piles of soil on the surface.

Mole emerging from a hole

Southern Hairy-nosed Wombat

Throwing their weight around

Wombats have been known to use their bulk to crush intruders against the sides of their burrows.

The Meerkat network

Meerkats are members of the mongoose family found in southern Africa's Kalahari Desert. As protection from predators, Meerkats live in large networks of burrows. The burrows have many entry and exit points so that at the first sign of danger the Meerkats can quickly scramble underground. To further help Meerkats stay safe, one or two will act as sentries while the rest of the 20 or so clan members forage.

Bulldozers of the bush

Their stocky shape and habit of barging through fences and other obstacles have led to these Australian marsupials being called 'the bulldozers of the bush'. Wombats use their sharp claws and powerful forelimbs to dig burrows, which can link up to form large warrens. Wombat burrows can be up to 30 metres (100 feet) long and are used during the day for resting and keeping out of sight. Wombats sometimes share their burrows but more usually spend their underground hours alone.

Meerkats

29

Butterflies and Moths

Butterflies, the most studied of all flying insects, are well known and much admired for their colourful wing patterns. Moths are less popular but there are many more of them—of the 165,000 species fluttering around, about 28,000 are butterflies and the rest are moths. Like many insects, butterflies can be found in almost all environments but are most common and diverse in the tropics. Many move to somewhere warmer during the winter months, undertaking massive migrations, while some don't travel far from 'home' at all.

Butterflies versus moths

Moths and butterflies are similar creatures with similar life styles and cycles but there are a few major differences between the two. Butterflies are usually active during the daytime and are often observed fluttering from flower to flower. Moths are nocturnal and usually have much duller and less patterned wings and feathery antenna. The two also have different resting poses— butterflies put their impressive wings together up over their bodies, while moths lay their wings flat.

Being a butterfly

Like many insect species, butterflies and moths reach adulthood in a series of dramatic changes. They start off as an egg, often laid on a leaf. When the larva hatches into a caterpillar it eats almost constantly, moulting its old skin many times. The next step is its transformation into a pupa, which is a resting stage where it remains protected inside a cocoon. Finally, the adult butterfly emerges ready to start the cycle all over again.

Monarch Butterfly perched on a flowerhead

A fairly fluid diet

Along with bees, butterflies and moths are important pollinators of flowering plants. Most adult butterflies use their proboscis to reach nectar, while earlier in their lives, when at the caterpillar stage, they dined mostly on leaves. A few caterpillar and butterfly species live off animal fluids, such as the harvester butterfly, which uses its proboscis to pierce the bodies of other insects so it can suck up their internal fluids.

Colour and movement

Tiny overlapping scales provide the brilliant colours and complex patterns of many butterfly species. Though they help in finding a mate, the shapes and colours are not there just to make butterflies look pretty. Camouflage is the purpose of the colouring on some, while others have patterns that look like eyes to fool predators into thinking that they're being watched. Bright colours in nature also often indicate that something isn't good to eat, making predators think twice about taking a taste test.

A coat of many colours

All moths fly at night, right? Wrong! Not the Joseph's Coat Moth (*Agarista agricola*), which flies about by day. Judging by its bright colours (it's named after Joseph's coat of many colours) and slow flight it probably tastes awful. The caterpillars feed on relatives of grapes and are brightly banded in black, white and orange—colours that warn off predators.

Moth and cocoons

Going, going ...

Many of the more spectacular butterfly species are in danger from over-collecting, while others face risks from habitat loss.

Rescuing the Richmond Birdwing

The Richmond Birdwing (*Ornithoptera richmondia*), one of Australia's largest butterflies, was in danger of extinction. This was partly because its rainforest habitat was being destroyed, and also because it often mistakenly laid its eggs on an introduced species of plant that poisoned them. Luckily people in north-east NSW and south-east Queensland began a campaign to save bushland and plant native Aristolochia vines for the butterflies, whose numbers have increased as a result.

C Care of Young

The survival of a species relies on enough individuals living long enough to reproduce. Since all animals go through a stage where they are too young to breed, the care of the young can be critical in giving them the chance to reach breeding age. Some animals, especially insects, reptiles and fish, are born in such large numbers that care is rarely given or needed—enough will survive to reach maturity. With many other animals though all offspring are precious, and are treated as such.

Fish families

You probably don't first think of fish when it comes to animal families. Usually fish just deposit their eggs and then swim away. One large group, however, the cichlids—with over 1500 species, including sunfish and angelfish—make very protective parents. Both sexes play their part, with the male often patrolling the territory and chasing intruders away while the female tends to the eggs and, once they have hatched, takes the fry out foraging.

Caring for the small fry

Parental care is common among spiders, scorpions, crustaceans, centipedes, molluscs, worms and jellyfish.

Naked, blind and helpless

While few egg-laying reptiles provide care for their young—most just lay and leave—nearly all bird species provide protection and food. Many bird hatchlings emerge from the egg blind, featherless and helpless and need parental care to survive. The level of care can vary widely—some birds just bring food until the young are old enough to fend for themselves while others, such as oystercatchers, need to teach the chicks special skills, like how to open up oysters—a lesson that can take months.

Brand-new duckling

Bringing up baby bugs

Insects are not often thought of for their child-rearing abilities and most species invest little time looking after larvae. But some beetle and bug species do their best to help the young reach adulthood. They will guard the eggs and emerging nymphs, often sheltering them with their bodies. Some try to deter or distract predators or bring food to the young. Some insects will even sacrifice themselves to a predator to allow the young time to escape.

Male water bugs carrying eggs on their backs

Mammal mums

Though mammals are not the only animals that care for their young, they are the group that most often devotes time and energy into raising offspring. Mammals have very dependent young, with most species requiring the care, shelter, food and protection of a parent, usually the mother, while they are growing up. Many mammal mums will put themselves in harm's way to protect their offspring, but the survival instinct is strong and in a 'do or die' situation most species will abandon the young to save themselves.

Lion mother with cubs

Carnivores

The word 'carnivore' is often used to describe all meat-eating animals. But strictly speaking, not all carnivores are meat-eaters. In science, 'carnivore' refers to the members of the Order Carnivora, a diverse group of animals that have one thing in common—four molar teeth that slice like scissors through flesh. Sharp claws and large, thick skulls are also common features, but beyond that, the 280 or so mammals classed as carnivores come in a range of shapes and sizes.

A mink stands over its prey, a mallard duck

Meat-eating plants
Some plants are also carnivores and will trap and digest insects and other small animals.

Meat-loving mustelids

The mustelid family contains many of the smallest, but toughest, hunters found within the carnivore group. The 65 species of mustelids, including otters, ferrets and stoats, are found all over the globe except for Australia and Antarctica. Using their highlydeveloped sense of smell to locate prey, the lean and flexible bodiesy of most mustelids allows them to pursue small mammals with speed and agility.

The vegetarian carnivore

Because of their ancient relatives and the shape of their teeth, giant pandas are classed as carnivores. But nowadays those teeth spend a lot more time biting bamboo than they do munching meat. Pandas will eat insects, small mammals and even fish if the opportunity arises, but overall they have adapted to a vegetarian lifestyle with bamboo making up nearly 100 per cent of their diet.

Black bear eating berries

Fruit and flesh

Many of the best known carnivores feed almost exclusively on meat. These include the dog and cat families, and the mustelid family, which includes badgers, weasels and ferrets. Bears are carnivores, but—with the exception of the polar bear—they can and will eat a variety of other foods. American black bears get the bulk of their nutrition from berries, nuts and other plant material, while sloth bears survive mostly on insects.

Swift seals

When you think of carnivores you usually don't think of sea creatures. But seals, sea lions and walruses, known collectively as pinnipeds, are all carnivores. Because they spend much of their time in the sea, pinnipeds prey mainly on fish, crabs and other aquatic animals. However, with a carnivore as fierce and strong as a leopard seal around, almost any creature unlucky enough to be in the water at dinner time could find itself on the menu.

Seal hunting fish

Cats

There are 37 species of cats; carnivores that range from the domestic cat to big cats such as lions, leopards, tigers and jaguars. Cats eat very little that isn't meat. Since 'meat' mostly moves, the members of the cat family need to be very skilful hunters to ensure a steady supply. Sharp senses and fast reflexes, along with an ability to silently stalk their prey, place cats among the world's best hunters.

The feline family

There is great diversity of size amongst cats, or felines as they are also known. They range from the tiny two kilogram kodkod of South America to the 225 kilogram (200 pound) African lion. But the basic shape remains the same, as does much of their behaviour. A domestic cat stalking something through the backyard is using the same senses and instincts as a jaguar in the jungle or a puma on the prairie.

The big 'big cats'

Big cats are usually classed as the four species within the Panthera genus—the lion, leopard, tiger and jaguar. These are the only cats that are able to roar, though the jaguar rarely chooses to. A broader definition of 'big cats' also includes the cheetah, puma and smaller leopard species such as the snow leopard. Big cats are able to roar because of their long larynx. Having the longest larynx lets the lion make by far the loudest roar.

Male African lion

Here puss, puss, puss

The animals that most of us think of when we think of 'cats', were first domesticated about 10,000 years ago in western Asia. Since then cats have had a close association with humans, winning affection for their skilful hunting of rats and mice and the companionship they provide. But it is not all good—of the 1000 or so species that the domestic cat can prey on, many are small native animals.

Fast felines

The cheetah is the world's fastest land animal. When running at full blast cheetahs can hit nearly 100 kilometres (62 miles) an hour, but can only maintain this speed for a minute, max, before they tire.

Domestic cat

Small, slender, swift

Somewhere between our 'domestic short-hair' pet moggies and the lion—king of the jungle—there are a heap of other felines to be found around the world. Many wild cats have beautiful striped, spotted and mottled coats to add camouflage to their already impressive hunting abilities. Many of the small cats such as ocelots and lynxes are mostly jungle or forest dwellers, but deserts and mountains also provide a habitat for some species.

Black panther

Coral Reefs

Corals are ancient organisms that first appeared over 400 million years ago, evolving into their reef building forms over the last 25 million years. Corals are part of the Cnidarian phylum, which includes sea anemones and jellyfish. They are actually very small creatures known as polyps. The polyps secrete limestone, which forms a hard skeleton so that as the polyps grow and divide, they lay the foundations for a coral reef, a constantly growing and changing collection of creatures.

Coral coverage

Coral reefs cover an estimated total of nearly 300,000 square kilometres (116 000 square miles) worldwide.

Plenty of fish in these seas

The only habitat that contains more species than a coral reef is tropical rainforest. Reefs provide shelter for many small fish and invertebrates that would otherwise have no place to hide. The reefs of Southeast Asia and Australia have the greatest numbers of species, with over 4000 different creatures identified. And these are just the species we know about—scientists suggest that we have so far only named about 10 per cent of the invertebrates living amongst coral reefs.

Reefs' needs

Coral reefs need very certain circumstances in order to be able to survive and thrive. These include shallow, warm waters, such as found in many parts of the tropics, and few nutrients in the water. Nutrients are bad news for coral reefs as they promote the growth of algae, which can 'suffocate' the coral. A process of recycling of nutrients between corals and other organisms in the water means that coral reefs can thrive in nutrient poor waters.

Great Barrier Reef

A Great Barrier Reef

Australia's Great Barrier Reef is the only living thing that can be seen from space—a system 2500 kilometres (1550 miles) long and 350,000 square kilometres (135 000 sqaure miles) in area, made from millions of corals. The reef provides a habitat for thousands of species of fish and other marine life. Because of this diversity, and for its sheer size and beauty, the reef is a World Heritage Site that has also been named one of the seven wonders of the natural world.

Fears and threats

Coral reefs are delicate systems with an easily upset balance. Natural disasters such as cyclones, diseases, predators of coral such as the Crown-of-thorns Starfish, pollution, the impact of tourism and the poaching of corals, even the mining of hard corals to make roads, can all cause damage beyond repair. One of the biggest threats facing reefs comes from global warming, as rising water temperatures often leads to coral bleaching, which can cause corals to die off in large numbers.

Bleached coral

Coral bleaching

Each coral usually contains only one species of zooxanthellae (tiny plants), which colours the coral, making the bright colours we see. When water gets too warm, great numbers of zooxanthellae are damaged by the heat and leave the coral, draining it not only of its vibrant colour, but also of essential nutrients. This is the cause of the coral bleaching that has been reported on the Great Barrier Reef.

Crocodiles and Alligators

Crocodiles and alligators, along with gharials and caimans, make up the 23 species of Crocodilians. Crocodilians have been around for about 220 million years and have many differences from their ancestors who lived during the dinosaur days. They are not the 'living fossils' many people think them to be. Surprisingly, though a crocodile doesn't resemble a cuckoo or an alligator look like a duck, the Crocodilians are more closely related to birds than they are to other reptiles.

Freshwater or Johnstone's Crocodile

Spot the difference

Crocodiles and alligators look similar but belong to different families. There are a few major differences between the two—one of these is dotted sensory organs on the skin—crocodiles have them all over, the other species just around their jaws. You can see these spots on a crocodile skin bag. They also have different teeth placement. But for quick recognition look at their heads—alligators and caiman have broad U-shaped jaws, while crocodile jaws make a pointed V.

Parenting skills

Like most reptiles, crocodiles and alligators lay eggs, anywhere from a dozen to 50 of them. Crocodilians make nests for the eggs from either mounds of plant matter or pits in the sand. In some species the mother guards the nests, which she opens up when the eggs are ready to hatch. She then carries the hatchlings in her mouth to a pre-prepared nursery pond. Despite this care, about nine out of ten hatchlings will fall prey to something bigger— sometimes even their dad!

American Alligators (*Alligator mississipiensis*)

The alligator bounces back

By the 1960s American Alligators were in trouble—the numbers of this once common south-eastern swamp dweller had fallen so low that the government listed them as endangered. The protection this gave caused a quick reversal in the alligators' fortunes—within 20 years numbers had risen to 800,000 and the alligator was common enough to come off the critical list. Now in fact some hunting is allowed in certain areas to keep population under control.

Underground living

The critically endangered Chinese alligator builds and lives in a system of water-filled underground burrows, complete with airholes for breathing.

Surprise, surprise!

Crocodiles mostly eat fish but they will hunt land animals at waterholes. They sneak in close to the shore, just beneath the water's surface, barely visible. With a sudden explosive burst from the water they grab the drinking prey by its snout or a leg. Then they drag or flip the animal into the water and spin it around in a 'death roll'. This quick kill reduces the chance of the prey escaping or of its flailing hooves or horns injuring the crocodile.

Crustaceans

There are around 50,000 species of crustaceans—arthropods found mainly in aquatic environments. Crustaceans range in size from miniscule krill to enormous spider crabs, and occupy just about every aquatic niche. In between the tiny and the mighty, there are many others—prawns, lobsters, crayfish, crabs and barnacles are all crustaceans. Like insects, crustaceans have segmented bodies, jointed legs and an exoskeleton, which can be a thin and flexible coating or a hard protective shell.

All shrimps and sizes

Crustaceans come in all shapes and sizes—from tiny shrimp and land-based wood lice to the four-metre leg span of Japanese spider crabs. Though not as broad, American lobsters are hefty, weighing just over 20 kilograms (44 pounds). At the other end of the scale come the water fleas and brine shrimp, measuring under a millimetre. Krill are small crustaceans that swim in swarms of many millions—which is just as well as a blue whale eats about 40 million krill a day!

Unkind cut

The swift skin-splitting strike of the Mantis Shrimp can slice a finger to the bone in less than a second—it is one of the fastest animal movements measured.

Land lubber lice

Wood lice are a minority group—land-dwelling species in a group of water lovers. Like other crustaceans they have gills, not lungs, so they tend to live in dark, damp places that supply enough moisture for them to breathe. Most of the 3000 species of wood lice are nocturnal, feeding on rotting plant matter in their sheltered soggy habitats. Common names we have given to wood lice include armadillo bugs, doodlebugs and roly-polys, roll-up bugs and slaters.

Eyes and mouths

Most crustacean heads have two antennae, a pair of eyes that are often set on stalks, and three mouths. As they swim, crawl and burrow around their environment they use these to navigate, see and eat. Many crustaceans are scavengers and get by on the little leftovers from the ocean's big life and death struggles. Others do their own catching and killing or are parasites while some follow a vegetarian lifestyle and feed on algae and other green plants.

The risk of renovating

Exoskeletons don't grow like our bones do, so as the crustacean gets bigger in size it must discard the shell and wait for a new one to form and harden. Most crustaceans feature as regularly on the menus of other underwater animals as they do at seafood restaurants, so this period can be particularly dangerous for a crustacean. But most are not totally defenceless—crabs and shrimp can use their powerful claws for both attack and defence.

Dogs

Dogs are carnivorous members of the Canidae family, which contains 34 species of dogs, wolves, jackals, foxes and coyotes. Most wild dog species live in grassland areas where they catch their prey with a sudden pounce or a long pursuit. Being very social animals, most canines live in packs that can range from a few individuals to dozens of dogs. Packs are maintained by a pecking order and by much sight, sound and smell based communication between the members.

Hunters on the horizon

Few predators arouse the response in prey animals that a pack of African wild dogs on the hunt will do. Zebras and antelopes are off and running as soon as they see these medium-sized pack dwellers on the horizon. This is because wild dogs will chase their prey for many kilometres, taking it in turns to run at the front of the pack. When the prey finally tires out it is quickly brought down for the kill.

Tame or domestic?

'Tame' does not mean the same thing as 'domesticated'. Individual wild animals can often be tamed by close and regular contact with humans but this would not apply to all the members of their species.

The undomesticated Dingo

Dingoes are well known as the native dog of Australia, but they originated in South-East Asia and can still be found in that region. Most likely brought over by traders around 4000 years ago, the Dingo quickly became associated with Australia's indigenous people. They used Dingoes to help with hunting and as companions, though they are not easily domesticated. Dingoes share features with both wolves and dogs, but unlike those animals the Dingo cannot bark, it can only howl.

Dingo

The cunning coyote

The coyote is a medium-sized native dog of North America. It usually lives and travels in small packs, but often hunts in pairs, targeting small mammals along with birds, large insects and a range of reptiles. Coyotes also kill many smaller domesticated animals, leading to an uneasy long-term relationship with humans. But this hasn't put them off—coyotes are adaptable and often thrive in suburbs and even cities with an estimated 2000 living in the Chicago area.

Coyote pups

A dog and his human

Our best friend

The domestic dog has been many things to many people for many thousands of years. First domesticated sometime between 14,000–9000 years ago, dogs have been willing workers for centuries, guarding us and our domestic animals, being used as beasts of burden or assistants in hunting, providing us with 'friendship', fur and food. Believed to have split from their wolf ancestors around 100,000 years ago, there are now an estimated 400 million domestic dogs spread over 800 breeds.

Domesticated Animals

Domesticated animals are those that humans have caught, tamed and bred over the centuries. We use domesticated animals for many different things. Cattle, poultry and sheep are used for milk, wool, eggs or meat. Horses, once used for labour, are now mostly used for sport and recreation. Dogs, cats, rabbits and cage birds are used for companionship. For many animals, their use to humans has helped ensure their survival, as it is in our interests to keep them healthy and protected from the dangers they would face in the wild.

Humans rely heavily on the cattle industry

A brief history lesson

Domestication of different animals took place at different times and in different places making it hard to pin down exact dates for any particular species. Most animals were domesticated in prehistoric times so the archaeological record is used to get some idea of when we first formed an association with an animal. Times can range from around 18,000–10,000 years ago for pigs, dogs, sheep, goats and cattle, to just a few thousand years back for domesticated birds such as ducks and geese.

Chickens have long been part of human life

Good breeding

When humans domesticate animals for a particular purpose they often try to add to the animal's usefulness by carefully choosing which ones they use for breeding. The many different breeds of sheep and cattle have been bred to provide thicker or finer quality fleeces, or to provide more meat or milk, depending on what they are to be used for. Horses are used for a range of reasons so they've been bred for speed, stamina, strength and temperament.

Horses have helped humans for many years

The helpful horse

Horses and humans have a long shared history, stretching back to between 6000–4000 years ago. Horses have been used in times of war to pull chariots and as both pack animals and to carry riders in cavalries. Though their military use is now minimal we still put the horse to work as a pack animal, for sporting events such as jumping and racing, and for the pleasure that horse riding provides many people.

E
Elephants

There are two species of elephant—African and Asian. The African Elephant is the largest land animal on Earth weighing a whopping 6.3 tonnes and standing up to four metres (13 feet) tall. All this weight is supported by solid legs and broad feet. An elephant's tusks are long teeth that keep on growing and they are used for digging for roots and water, stripping bark from trees, fighting and for defending themselves and the calves. Elephants can live for up to 70 years.

Elephants use their trunks to suck, spray, pick and carry

What's with the trunk?

An elephant's trunk, a joined upper lip and nose, is very sensitive and has over 100,000 muscles. It's also very useful for breathing and smelling, sucking up water or spraying it around and picking up and carrying objects, from a single blade of grass to large heavy logs. Trunks can be used in defence or attack and are much used in social contact. Elephants can make noises with their trunks, from trumpets to whistles to roars, and rumbles so low our ears can't hear them.

All you can eat

Animals the size of elephants need a lot of fuel to keep them going, so it's no surprise they spend about 18–20 hours a day eating or looking for the 150 kilograms (330 pounds) of food each individual will consume. Grasses make up half their diet, followed by just about any other vegetation around—leaves, roots, bark and twigs, sometimes seeds and fruits. Elephants travelling for food can also stir up a feast of disturbed insects and reptiles for many small grassland birds.

Beasts of burden

Asian Elephants have been used as beasts of burden for thousands of years though males can be unpredictable and the species is not totally domesticated.

Emotional elephants

Elephants are emotional and individuals in a herd have many varied and close connections. When herds that have been separated are reunited the elephants seem to show delight. Excited running around, lots of trumpeting and squealing and much touching with their trunks are typical reactions. Elephants also seem to be able to recognise themselves in a mirror, and have an understanding of death, appearing to 'grieve' when they lose a family member.

Family life

It's the females that make up elephant herds—from up to 40 mothers and daughters, sisters and aunties, and their young. Males live alone or in small groups, coming and going from the herds from time to time. Females share the babysitting duties and will band together to protect young elephants from danger. Some elephant herds wander a lot, others don't, with home ranges covering anything from about 20 square kilometres (7 square miles) to up around 3000 (1200 square miles).

A herd of African Elephants running

Endangered Animals

There'd barely be a beast in this book that doesn't have a close relative facing extinction. In all major groups—fish and reptiles, insects, mammals and birds—there are creatures just clinging on to survival. Poaching and pollution, uncontrolled hunting and overfishing can all push a species over the extinction edge. But the biggest threat facing thousands of creatures, both amazing animals that we admire and things we haven't even found yet, is habitat loss, because nothing can survive for long without somewhere suitable to live.

Vanishing habitat
All of the rainforest of the Philippines is gone and so is 90 per cent of the West African jungle.

Golden Lion Tamarin

You have to have a habitat

All animals are locked into a relationship with the habitat where they live. They have adapted to find food and shelter within it, along with all the other plant and animal species, and together they make up each habitat's community. Communities are linked by food webs and many of the organisms rely on each other for survival. As many varied habitats continue to be damaged or destroyed by human activities, so are many varied animals left with nowhere else to go.

Working it out

Animals at risk are ranked from 'least concern' to 'critically endangered'. And it's not far from critical to the last label—'extinct'. Each year the World Conservation Union publishes a 'Red List' of endangered animals. It currently lists over 12,000 species, including one in four mammals, one in eight birds and about a third of all amphibians. And that's just the ones we know about—many animals rely on each other through complex connections so the loss of one species affects many others.

Rhinos north and south

Efforts to save endangered animals can sometimes be success stories, at other times make sad reading. Two sub-species of Africa's white rhinos, the northern and southern, have tales with very different endings. The northern numbered a few thousand in the 1960s, but poaching has reduced numbers to around 30, making it the most endangered large mammal on Earth. The southern, thought extinct 100 years ago, has been rebuilt from a 40 member herd that survived the slaughter to now number around 11,000.

Tigers in trouble

In 1900 there were about 100,000 tigers in the wild. Now there are only 2500—there are more tigers in zoos than in the jungle. Hunted for their fur and for 'fun', the tiger came close to being a casualty of the ongoing struggle between our world and that of wild animals. Tigers are now protected in most countries and trading in their skins is banned. Even so, one of the planet's most perfect predators remains very much at risk.

Siberian Tiger

Extinctions

Extinction is when a species of animal ceases to exist altogether, both in captivity and in the wild. Extinction can be a natural occurrence caused by changes to environments, but it can be rapidly sped up by deliberate, thoughtless or accidental human activities. Extinction is usually a slow process, especially when it is a result of nature 'taking its course', but when humans get involved the speed with which a species can cease to exist can be frightfully fast.

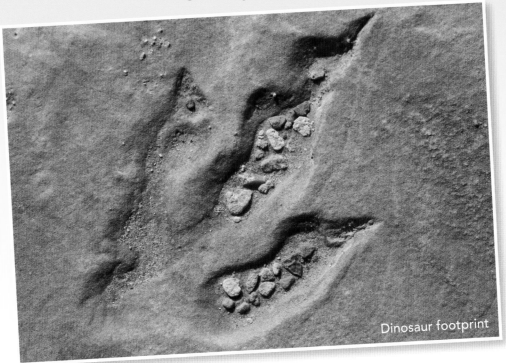
Dinosaur footprint

Dead as a dinosaur

The most famous mass extinction is that of the dinosaurs. The exact number of species is not known, because information is based on what bones are found, but whatever the number they dominated animal planet for nearly 150 million years. Then, along with 70 per cent of all other animal life, they were wiped out 65 million years ago. The cause of this cataclysm is hotly debated, but climate change, volcanic activity and the impact of a massive meteor crashing into the Earth may all have played a part.

Ancient extinctions

Extinctions are nothing new and have often occurred in the past. At the end of the last glacial period, or ice age, about 10,000–15,000 years ago, a massive extinction of a host of giant marsupials and other mammals, birds and reptiles took place. Many of these creatures were termed 'megafauna' because of their huge size. Scientists don't know exactly why, but the likely cause is a combination of climate change and the impact of human hunting and habitat altering.

Passenger Pigeon

Once plentiful passengers

When a pigeon called Martha died in 1914 her species went with her. When Europeans colonised North America there were as many as five billion passenger pigeons—one flock could be kilometres (miles) wide, over five kilometres (3 miles) long, and take days to pass overhead. Habitat loss had an impact but it was hunting that wiped out the passenger. 'Sportsmen' destroyed the last large flock in 1896, well aware there were no more. From there the finish came fast—within 15 years the passenger pigeon was extinct.

Domestic breeds in danger

Some domestic animal breeds are in danger of extinction as farmers concentrate on those breeds which supply the most meat, milk or wool.

Tasmania's targeted tiger

Until recently the thylacine, or Tasmanian Tiger, was the largest carnivorous marsupial. Though it had disappeared from mainland Australia around 3000 years ago it was the top predator on the island on Tasmania. Large numbers were hunted down because of a reputation as sheep-killers and though people hope it may cling on in remote and rugged regions there have been no confirmed sightings of this once widespread animal since the 1930s.

Thylacine

Wrecking the rainforests

One of the biggest challenges facing thousands, maybe millions, of animals is the ongoing destruction of forest habitats. Over the last 8000 years humans have cleared nearly 80 per cent of the world's forests. Tropical rainforests are the most species rich environment on the planet—the Amazon region alone is home to more than a third of the entire world's species, but it is being cleared for logging and grazing at a rate of nearly 25,000 square kilometres (10 000 square miles) a year.

It's getting warm in here

A major challenge facing all the planet's plants and animals, including us, is global warming. The majority of scientists agree that the planet is warming and that our burning of fossil fuels is a major contributor. Even a rise of a few degrees could have major impacts as most animals have adapted to specific environments. Climate-driven changes to many habitats could spell the end for the inhabitants—the polar bear is just one creature in immediate danger from global warming.

Amazon rainforest—slashed and burned

Wildlife wipe-out

If we don't get active the destruction of the dinosaurs won't be the best known extinction event—the one we are living through will. Africa's apes have seen a 50 per cent population decline and two-thirds of turtle species could be gone in 20 years, along with many marsupials and nearly half of Asia's animal species. There are many species we know little or nothing about, and some scientists suggest that we could be losing something every 20 minutes or so— that's nearly 30,000 species each and every year.

Endangered African Gorilla

Kenai National Wildlife Refuge
U.S. FISH AND WILDLIFE SERVICE
DEPARTMENT OF THE INTERIOR

Haunted by hunters

The Saiga Antelopes of central Asia numbered more than a million just over ten years ago. The impact of hunting with automatic weapons has seen their population drop by over 90 per cent to about 30,000.

Pressure from people

As the world's population increases and developing countries strive for a better quality of life, land—particularly in these developing nations—becomes increasingly sought after and rare. Forests and grasslands are cleared for farming, stripped for timber or dug up for minerals. All these activities alter, damage or destroy animal habitats. And the pressure will keep building, with Africa expected to double its population over the next 50 years.

Thinking of the future

There were none in the 1870s and there are now over 400,000 worldwide. Wildlife reserves now cover 10 per cent of the earth on Earth, the size of China and India combined. Reserves where hunting is banned and the habitat left undisturbed are one of the best ways of preserving wildlife. But there are many factors to be considered in setting up these essential safe spots, including the impact of and on humans living nearby, and controlling poaching and other illegal activities.

F Feral Animals

Feral animals are domesticated creatures that have somehow returned to the wild. Feral animals are usually considered pests and are often hunted, trapped and poisoned. This is because they tend to damage the environment and prey on native species or successfully compete with them for food. Feral predators such as cats and foxes often have the edge over native species, which have evolved without defences against hunters that really shouldn't be in their environment.

The wild side of life

The ease and extent with which a domesticated animal turns feral varies widely. Some herbivores such as goats easily adapt to life outside the fences and survive without having much of a struggle. Sheep and goats are closely related and were both domesticated about 12,000 years ago, but sheep are more accident and injury prone and have little chance against predators so they stick to the safety of protected paddocks.

Escapees all over the world

Most countries have feral animals to deal with including Australian possums in New Zealand and wallabies that have reportedly escaped and gone wild in parts of Europe.

No introduction necessary

Introduced animals are not the same as feral creatures. Rabbits and foxes were introduced to Australia mainly so early settlers could hunt them, while animals such as rats and mice just came along for the cruise. Sometimes animals are deliberately introduced to try and make a change to the environment. Usually they do but most often it's for the worse, as with the cane toad which was introduced to Australia to eat a pest and has become a much bigger one.

Cane toads

Those feral Australians

The island continent of Australia is a big place with a host of habitats that are sparsely populated by people but home to a huge variety of native species. These days the 'locals' have to share their habitats with invaders of all shapes and sizes—members of almost every animal species introduced to Australia has gone feral. These include the usual suspects such as cats, dogs, pigs, goats and horses, but some surprising feral Australians are camels and water buffalo.

Wild mother pig with young

Mountain mustangs and bush brumbies

Both Australia and the USA are home to large herds of 'wild' horses. These are known as brumbies in Australia and mustangs in America. In the US some of the herds are protected as living symbols of the wilderness. Because of this image and our affection for horses, the culling of wild herds raises strong emotions, but wild horses can cause much damage to the environment as well as competing with livestock for grazing land.

Brumbies roam free in the Australian Outback

Fish

The 25,000 separate species of fish together make up over half of all the vertebrates on Earth. Fish are cold-blooded aquatic animals found in nearly all watery habitats from lakes and streams to the coldest and deepest oceans. Fish have many aquatic adaptations including gills that allow oxygen to be extracted from water, scale-covered bodies shaped like torpedoes that allow them to swim with ease and speed, and fins that they use to propel and stabilise themselves.

Those fin things

Most fish have fins, which come in a range of shapes and sizes depending on the job they do. Dorsal fins are found on a fish's back. Numbering up to three, they assist with sudden stops and turns and help prevent the fish from rolling over. Pectoral fins are located on either side of the body and help maintain balance and provide a lifting force. Movement of the tail fin, along with that of the entire body, is used to propel most fish through the water.

Anglerfish

Fished out

Many fish species are at risk because of overfishing for human food, pollution and other forms of habitat damage.

Deep sea divers

Some of the most unusual fish are the rarely encountered deep sea species. Unable to survive outside of their oxygen-poor, low-lit and extremely high water pressure environments, most of what we know about them has been discovered by examining dead specimens. We do know that some of their adaptations include large eyes and nostrils for locating prey in dark water, and light-producing organs that are used as lures to entice prey to come that little bit closer.

An exception to every rule

Though fish are usually classed as cold blooded, some species such as tuna, swordfish and some sharks are able to raise their own body temperature. Many freshwater species, such as the lungfish, are an exception to the 'oxygen from water' rule and are also able to breathe via the air. And while when we think of fish we assume they'll be swimming in water, some species such as mudskippers spend more time on dry land than they do in the water.

Dragons and horses

Seahorses and sea dragons might not look like fish, but they are. Found throughout the world's subtropical and tropical oceans, sea horses tend to live in mangrove areas, sea grass meadows or on coral reefs. Seahorses use their prehensile tails to cling onto rocks and avoid being washed away by currents. Leafy sea dragons are well-camouflaged relatives of the seahorse that are found in Australian waters. Both creatures are predators without teeth, swallowing small prey whole.

A group of mudskippers on a tidal flat

Weedy Seadragon

Frogs and Toads

Frogs and toads are semi-aquatic amphibians found in all but the world's coldest regions. Of the 5000 or so species of frogs and toads, 80 per cent are found in the tropics. Frogs and toads have long, springy hind legs, no tail and moist skins. They vary enormously in size, ranging from a Brazilian Toad that measures under one centimetre to the African Goliath Frog, which reaches lengths of 30 centimetres and weighs over three kilograms (7 pounds).

What's with all the noise?

Anyone who has spent time by a creek or dam during spring will have heard all number of male frogs croaking in the hopes of finding a mate. Each species has its own distinct call and the females judge them to determine if the noisy male would make a fit mate. Unfortunately for the frogs, the females aren't the only ones with ears tuned in to the male's self-advertising—the croaks also attract bats, birds and other predators.

It flies through the trees

The rainforest-dwelling Java Flying Frog uses the skin between its toes to glide between trees and parachute down to lower branches.

Polluted creeks have caused frog numbers to decline

The croaking frogs

Frogs and other amphibians across the world have been dying off in large numbers. The cause of this population crash is not known for sure, but it could be related to a number of environmental changes. Frogs are well-known to be very sensitive to pollution in their environments and this, along with the use of pesticides and insecticides, could be one of the major contributors. Global warming and habitat loss could also be involved in this world-wide population decline.

From tadpole to frog

The life of a frog begins in the water with the laying of eggs, which will hatch into tadpoles after about two weeks. Tadpoles live exclusively in the water, using gills to breathe and a tail for swimming. As they grow, tadpoles lose their tails and develop lungs for breathing on land in a process that takes about four weeks. By the time six weeks have passed the tadpole has become a frog.

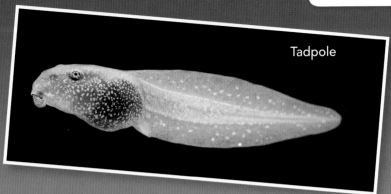
Tadpole

What's in a name?

Together, frogs and toads are called anurans. Though toads also return to the water to lay their eggs, they tend to be found more often on land than the frogs. Other differences include the warty skin found on many toad species, poison glands behind their eyes and the fact that frogs have teeth while toads do not. But both frogs and toads use their long sticky tongues to catch the insects and other small creatures that make up their diet.

A toad—warts and all

61

H Herbivores

Herbivores are animals that get all of their energy from the plants and grasses that they eat. Unlike omnivores, herbivores are exclusively 'vegetarian' with digestive systems that allow them to digest plant matter. Some herbivores eat only grasses while others depend on fruit, flowers, leaves or pollen. Because plants provide much less energy than meat, herbivores spend much of their day eating in order to get all the nutrients that they need.

Plants as prey

In a way plants are the herbivore's 'prey'. Unlike most plant-eaters, plants can't run away but that doesn't mean they are totally defenceless. One effective plant defence system is the use of chemicals that can make a plant taste unpleasant or cause illness in any creature that consumes it. While meat-eaters can rarely feed without killing the meat supply, some plants benefit from being grazed on as this encourages new growth.

All shapes and sizes
Not all herbivores have four legs and a tail—earthworms are herbivorous scavengers that help break down dead plant material.

A huge Cape Buffalo

The not-so-harmless herbivores

People often believe that only carnivores are dangerous, but many herbivores are large and powerful and will attack a human if they feel they or their young are threatened. Most large carnivores avoid humans, so in wildlife reserves where people are visiting, such as Yellowstone National Park, people are much more likely to tangle with a bison than a wolf. In Africa, three of the five species classed as the most dangerous to hunt are herbivores—rhinos, Cape buffalos and elephants.

A bull eating grass

Making the most of a meal

Herbivores such as cattle, sheep, goats, camels, giraffes, deer and antelopes are known as ruminants. These creatures have four stomachs, the first of which is known as the rumen. In the rumen, swallowed plant matter is broken down. This semi-digested food is then regurgitated by the animal and re-chewed, to further break down the food. Once the plant matter, known as cud, has been re-chewed it is swallowed again to be fully digested.

Something for everyone

On the African savannah more than a dozen different grazing species might roam the same area. To reduce competition for food many species eat different parts of the same plants. Zebras often arrive first at fresh grazing grounds and their teeth are designed to let them easily eat the longest, toughest parts of the grass. They are followed by the wildebeests and other antelopes, which concentrate more on the young and tender shoots. And giraffes are designed to eat the leaves nobody else can reach!

African herbivores at a watering hole

Hippopotamus and Rhinoceros

Hippos and rhinos are two of Africa's biggest, bulkiest herbivores, but they lead very different lives. The semi-aquatic hippos, whose closest living relatives are thought to be whales, spend much time in the water, while rhinos rarely leave land. Both can grow to massive sizes—the hippo to a length of over four metres and a height of 1.5 metres (5 feet), while the rhino also reaches four metres plus in length and stands nearly two metres at the shoulder. But it's their bulk that most impresses—both commonly weigh over two tonnes.

Don't hamper the hippo

Hippopotamuses have a reputation—it's believed they kill more people in Africa than any other large animal and in the home of the lion, leopard and Nile crocodile, that's some distinction. Hippos can be very territorial and use their sharp tusk-like canine teeth to attack whatever threatens them or their young. People encounter hippos from boats or on riverbanks and since they are able to run at nearly 50 kilometres (30 miles) an hour an angry hippo can easily chase down a human.

Happy as a hippo in mud

Hippos are found in the lakes and rivers of Africa where groups of up to 40 spend their days in water or mud. Unable to sweat, hippos rely on liquids to keep cool and stop the thin outer layer of their thick skins drying out. Less territorial on land than in water, hippos emerge at dusk to spend up to five hours grazing on grasses. The ability to stay submerged for over five minutes is just one of the hippo's water-friendly adaptations.

A petite hippo?

The pygmy hippo might be smaller than the common hippo, but it's no slouch when it comes to size—pygmy hippos can reach nearly two metres in length and weigh nearly 300 kilograms.

White Rhinoceros

Black and white and brown

Of the five rhino species, two live in Africa and the other three in southern Asia. Easily recognised by their solid shape and one or two horns, rhinos have keen hearing and senses of smell but poor eyesight. This can lead to them charging towards real or imagined threats at speeds of 50 kilometres (30 miles) an hour. Despite their names, 'black' and 'white' rhinos are similar in colour and both are often coated in the brown mud they like wallowing in.

Rhinos in trouble

All of the five rhino species are in danger because of human activity. Three species are critically endangered, one is endangered and Africa's more abundant white rhinos are classed as vulnerable. Rhinos face this threat because of habitat loss and illegal hunting for their horns, considered a powerful ingredient in some traditional Asian medicines. The horn's natural use is as a weapon for fighting rivals or protecting the young from predators.

Hyenas

There are four species in the hyena family—the brown, spotted and striped hyenas and the Aardwolf. Though dog-like in appearance, hyenas are more closely related to cats. Striped hyenas can be found both in and out of Africa, stretching into parts of western Asia, but the other species are found in Africa only. A sloping spine, short hind legs and powerful jaws and teeth capable of crushing bone are features of the hyena.

Hyena packs are matriarchal

Unjustly accused

For many years hyenas were considered cowardly scavengers, quick to steal food from 'noble' animals such as leopards and lions. Now we know that hyenas hunt, catch and kill much of their food. If anything, hyenas are more likely to lose a kill to larger lions than the other way around. Lions and hyenas will often fight over a kill and whichever has the advantage of numbers usually gets the goods.

Girl power

Hyenas live in clans, groups that can contain just a few individuals or up to 80 members, as in some spotted hyena groups. These clans have a fixed pecking order in which the bigger and stronger adult females dominate the smaller male members. Organisations such as this where females dominate are known as matriarchal. The social relationships within these clans are very complex, and mostly communicated through a wide range of sounds and body language.

The ant-eating aardwolf

Smaller than the striped hyenas that they resemble, shy, nocturnal aardwolves are insect-eaters that use their long sticky tongues to get at termites and other small creatures. Like all members of the hyena family, aardwolves are clever creatures. Though an aardwolf can consume up to 200,000 termites a night, care is taken to not destroy the nest or gobble the lot, ensuring the aardwolf has a future food source.

All you can eat

Hyenas are one of the few mammals that are able to digest the skin and bones and hooves and horns of their prey.

The power of the pack

A fully grown hyena is quite capable of bringing down large prey on its own, but most hyena clans hunt as a pack when going after big game. Operating in much the same manner as African wild dogs, hyena packs chase prey over long distances until exhaustion and pack power brings it down. Hyena packs often seem to specialise in their choice of prey, with some clans targeting wildebeests while others nearly always head out to hunt zebras.

Hyena hunting pack

# Insects

Insects might be small, but there are plenty of them—there are over a million known species and about 10,000 new ones are identified each year. And that is just the tip of the iceberg—estimates of the total number of insect species range from two million to a whopping 10-30 million. And that is just the species—the number of insects alive at any given time has been estimated at around 10 quintillion—that's 10,000,000,000,000,000,000—a lot of zeros, and a lot of insects!

What makes an insect?

Though there is huge variety within the insect world certain features are shared by all species, including bodies that are divided into three segmented parts—the head, thorax and abdomen. Six jointed legs are another essential insect requirement, along with two antennae that are used as sensory devices. Finally, all insects have a hard exoskeleton, which provides them with protection without restricting their movement.

Green Cicada

Grow up!

Most insects share a similar life cycle where they progress from eggs to larvae or nymphs, then to pupae and finally reach adulthood. This process is known as metamorphosis and it can be either incomplete, in which the animal changes its body gradually; or complete, which involves a total body shape change. With incomplete metamorphosis nymphs hatch from the egg looking like smaller versions of the adult. They then go through up to five sheddings of their skin, finally reaching the adult stage.

Pests or pals?

Flying, stinging, biting and swarming insects are often considered a major pest by most people. It's true that many a picnic or wheat crop has been ruined by them, and some species do spread potentially deadly diseases. Most insects, however, cause humans no harm and in fact do them a lot of good—about three-quarters of the world's flowering plants rely on insects to pollinate them, so you could argue that we need insects a lot more than they need us.

Sheep Blowfly maggots

A sizeable stick

Some of the planet's biggest insects include the Giant Stick Insect of Malaysia that has been said to reach over 55 centimetres (21 inches).

Insects everywhere!

Insects are found right across the planet in the hottest and coldest, wettest and driest environments. This incredible insect success story is due to a number of factors. Being the only invertebrates able to fly has allowed insects to spread themselves out. Their small size means a great number can live in a small space and still have enough food and shelter. Insects' short life cycle, combined with large numbers of offspring means that new generations are constantly evolving and helping develop the huge diversity within the insect class.

Paper Nest Wasp

Invertebrates

Most invertebrates are small but what they lack in size they make up in numbers and diversity. Over 95 per cent of all known animal species are invertebrates—animals that have no spine or other bones or cartilage. Within the world of invertebrates there is huge variety, including squid, spiders, sponges, corals, jellyfish, crabs and insects. Invertebrates lack bones but all are supported by some form of skeleton despite how soft they might seem.

Tiger worms

Worms everywhere

A lot of the wrigglers we call 'worms' may not be worms at all—they might be worm-like crustaceans or other long slender invertebrates. There are four main types of worms: flatworms, ribbon worms, roundworms and segmented worms. The thousands of worm species are spread across the world, living in salt and fresh water and on land. Many are parasites, while others are predators or eat rotting vegetation. Most terrestrial worms live in soils.

Jellies that sting

Jellyfish are marine invertebrates that live in both salt and fresh water. Adult jellyfish have bell-like bodies with trailing tentacles. They move by drifting with the current or opening and closing their bodies to propel them through the water. In many species the tentacles are covered with stinging cells that trap, then paralyse or kill their diet of small fish and other invertebrates. These stinging cells are also used for defence as anyone stung by a Bluebottle at the beach knows only too well!

Seeing stars

Starfish can have as many as 40 suckered arms, though around five is more typical. However many they have, starfish use these arms to help them move across the sea bed as they hunt crustaceans. Starfish have two stomachs, one of which can be used to engulf prey that won't fit in their mouths. Able to re-grow lost arms, starfish can also regenerate from a single arm, as long as it still has some of the central body attached.

Termite towers

Termites are insect invertebrates. Though they are often called white ants, they belong to a different order to the true ants. Termites are social insects, living in large colonies that can contain millions of individuals. Most colonies are headed by an egg-laying queen who is attended and defended by the worker and solider termites. Workers provide much of the colony's food, which for most species consists of dead plant material such as wood.

Plant or animal?

Sea sponges were long thought to be plants but the 9000 odd species are in fact invertebrate animals.

The boneless Bluebottle Jellyfish

Kangaroos

Kangaroos are large, grass-eating marsupials found on the island continent of Australia. There are four species—the Red, Eastern and Western Greys, and the Antilopine Kangaroo of northern and north-western Australia. The Red Kangaroo is the largest, with males growing to a height of over 2 metres (7 feet). The females have a pouch in which they raise their young, known as joeys. Kangaroos tend to be most active at dusk and dawn, spending the hot daylight hours resting in the shade.

Black-footed Rock Wallaby

What's a wallaby?

Wallabies are a mixed group made up of the smaller relatives of kangaroos. There are about 60 species classed as wallabies, including the rock wallaby, nail-tail, pademelon, hare-wallaby and dorcopsis. Some wallaby species, usually the bigger, faster ones, share the grassland home of the kangaroos. Rock wallabies live in rugged terrain and are slower, but very agile. Wallaroos are smaller than kangaroos but bigger than wallabies while pademelons are small forest dwellers.

Climbing kangaroos

Tree kangaroos can be found in the tropical rainforests of Australia and New Guinea, especially in mountainous regions. They have stronger forelimbs and longer balancing tails than their ground-bound relatives. Longer claws and wider feet with rubbery soles also assist them to grip and climb. Though slow and clumsy on the ground these kangaroos are agile in the trees and can leap nine metres down to lower branches.

Tree kangaroo

Leaps and bounds

The only large animals that use hopping as a way of getting around, kangaroos move slowly most of the time. But when they need to kangaroos can really move, using their large feet and strong legs to reach speeds of over 60 kilometres (40 miles) an hour, jump three-metre fences and leap 12 metres (40 feet) in a single bound. Their long muscular tails help keep their balance during all this leaping and bounding.

Kick power

Male kangaroos will use their powerful hind legs to kick out at rivals during kangaroo confrontations.

Red Kangaroo

What a mob

Kangaroos are social creatures and live in groups that are known as mobs. Mobs can range in size from a few individuals to up to 50 or even more. Living in a mob may be a safety precaution, but since the extinction of the thylacine on the mainland, the only dangerous predators that kangaroos face are dingoes and a few feral species such as foxes and dogs.

L Leopards and Lions

Lions are the biggest of Africa's big cats, with the leopard coming in second. Both are carnivores of the Panthera genus, but there are many differences between the two. The leopard is easily recognised by its striking spots, while lions have plainer, sandy coloured coats and the male his impressive mane. Just because lions and leopards are related doesn't mean they get on. Predators compete, and lions will kill leopard cubs and even adults when the opportunity arises.

Pride life

Lions are unusual in living in large groups, known as prides—most cats are solitary. Prides are family affairs, made up of one or two males, about half a dozen related females and the cubs, which can range from newborns to almost fully grown adults. Prides provide protection, social interaction and more eyes, ears, noses, legs, claws and teeth to find, catch and kill prey. Males leave when they reach maturity to look for a pride they can try and take over.

Asiatic Lion

Learning about leopards

Leopards are solitary, seldom seen animals—by human visitors to Africa or, when the hunt is successful, their prey. Leopards hunt mostly at night, catching prey by sneaking up close and, after a sudden ambush, strangling it with a bite to the throat. The spots on the leopards' coat, called rosettes, become distinct as young leopards mature. To protect her cubs from predators, the mother leopard keeps them hidden in a den.

Picking your prey

Most predators will take whatever animals they can overpower, so the smaller leopard favours smaller prey than the large herbivores usually targeted by lion prides. Lions are always on the lookout for an easy meal and a kill causes a commotion, which attracts attention from dedicated scavengers like vultures. Leopards use their climbing ability to drag their prey into safe larders high in the trees, to avoid losing what has taken them a lot of effort to catch.

Leopard with a kill up a tree

A short life

Life can be short for lion cubs and come to a swift, savage end. Lionesses won't breed when they are raising young cubs. If a new male takes over a pride, his first instinct is to breed. In order to do this, the male immediately kills all the young cubs so that the pride's lionesses will accept him as a mate. The females will sometimes try to defend the cubs, but are no match for the much bigger male.

The bigger the hairdo the better

Male lions are the only cat to have a mane. The mane makes the lion look bigger and more intimidating when confronting other lions or competitors. Lionesses also seem to prefer the lions with the best head of hair!

Mammals

The earliest mammals were shrew-like creatures that lived about 200 million years ago and were the ancestors of the 4250 or so species currently existing. Mammals are a very diverse group in size, habitats and lifestyle, though they all share certain features. Mammals are warm blooded, give birth to live young that they feed on milk produced by the mother and have hair on their bodies. The main exceptions to these rules are the Australian platypus and echidna, both of which lay eggs instead of having live young.

The mammal mind

Mammals are the most intelligent of animals, at least in terms of how we human mammals judge intelligence. Dolphins and apes are well-known for their learning capabilities and even the lowly rat has shown intelligence when it comes to learning how to perform tasks. The size of an animal's brain may indicate how intelligent it is—many herbivores have relatively smaller brains than the predators that hunt them and have to be able to outwit their prey.

Even the lowly rat has shown intelligence

The adaptable mammal

Mammals are among the most adaptable animals on the planet, being found in all but the coldest, highest or deepest environments. Within these environments mammals also show huge diversity, ranging in size from tiny mice to massive whales and land animals such as elephants. Along with size diversity there is a wide range of lifestyles that includes arboreal, terrestrial and aquatic living, or combinations of these.

Mammals are adaptable—this Japanese macaque bathes in warm thermal pools to keep warm in its cold environment

Record rhino

The largest land mammal that ever lived was a hornless rhinoceros that is estimated to have stood five metres (16 feet) at the shoulder and have been 11 metres long (36 feet).

Mum's the word

Mammals live all sorts of lives, from a solitary existence to never leaving the safety of the group. One thing all have in common though is that they been raised by their mother and fed on her milk until they were old enough to find and eat solid foods. The period in which a mammal is dependent on the mother can vary wildly, from short periods for small creatures such as rodents, to years in the case of elephants, whales and humans.

It's all in the jaw

One thing that makes a mammal a mammal is that its lower jaw bone attaches directly to its skull. This jaw and bone structure, along with three inner ear bones, is present in all mammal species regardless of any other differences. All mammals also have hair or fur, which can completely cover the body or be there but barely noticeable, as in the sparse hair on whales and dolphins.

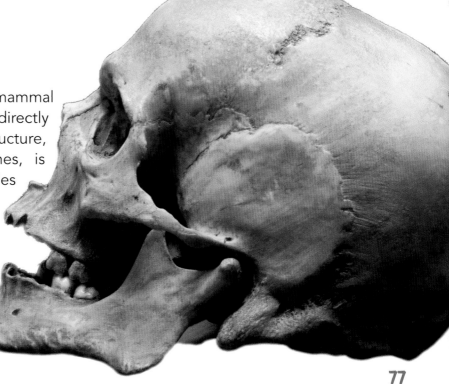

Marine Mammals

Streamlined bodies and limbs shaped like fins are shared adaptations that make marine mammals suited to life in the sea. They are also able to stay underwater for a long time. There are about 120 species of marine mammals, including seals, sea lions, walruses, whales and dolphins, sea otters and sea cows. While whales, dolphins and sea cows live an entirely aquatic life, walruses, seals and sea lions return to shore to breed and raise their young.

Underwater ability

The 30 or so species of seals and sea lions dive down, very deep, and stay underwater for a long time, up to a couple of hours. They can do this because their heartbeats slow down and their blood and muscles are used as internal oxygen storage tanks. Layers of blubber and a covering of hair insulate these underwater acrobats against the cold waters of the northern and southern seas where most live.

Sea lion pup

Fed and watered

Most marine mammals get the fresh drinking water they need from the food that they eat.

What's a walrus?

The walrus is in a family all its own, the Odobenidae family. Walruses are well known for their impressive tusks, up to a metre long. These are actually very long canine teeth, used for fighting between males; digging breathing holes in the ice; and hauling the heavy walrus body back up onto the ice. The tusks may also play a role in feeding, though the snout and strong sensitive whiskers play the major roles in keeping the walrus full of molluscs.

Ocean otters

Blubber keeps most marine mammals warm in icy waters, but sea otters have thick fur to keep the cold out. Humans have about 175–130 hairs per square centimetre (27-20 square inches) of skin—sea otters have 200,000. Sea otters spend nearly all their time in and on the water, floating on the surface to sleep, and can live in the ocean all the time if they choose. To get their mostly mollusc and crustacean diet they use rocks as tools to dislodge and crack shells.

Sea Otter

Underwater cows

Sea cow is another name for manatees and dugongs—aquatic herbivores that graze the sea grasses of the world's warm tropical and subtropical waters. Dugongs are ocean dwellers while manatees are more often found in estuaries and up rivers. Gentle, curious creatures, sea cows face their greatest threat from humans, who hunt them for meat. Protection can seem almost pointless because policing the endangered sea cows' habitat is very difficult.

Dugong mother and calf

Marsupials

Marsupials are unique for a number of reasons. The name 'marsupial' means pouched mammal, and all of the 300 or so species have this adaptation. Marsupials also have slower metabolisms and lower body temperatures than other mammals and slightly smaller brains. The pouched mammals include opossums, kangaroos and koalas, wombats, bandicoots and possums. Marsupials are divided into two groups—those found in the Americas and the 200 diverse species found across Australia, New Guinea and many nearby islands.

Miniature marsupials

Young marsupials are underdeveloped and tiny—most are no bigger than an insect—and totally defenceless. Born after very short gestation periods, newborns are known as neonates. The only well-developed limb on a neonate is a strong font claw. This is used to drag the neonate through their mother's fur to the protection of the pouch. Here, they will find a teat to suckle from and slowly develop inside the pouch.

The purpose of a pouch

Pouches provide protection from predators and the place for a neonate to feed and grow—young marsupials would not survive outside of it. Many joeys, as the young of kangaroos, wombats and wallabies are known, still spend a lot of time hanging around at home even after being weaned and will use their mother's pouch for warmth, sleeping, if they feel threatened, or for being transported from place to place.

Newborn kangaroo in mother's pouch

Efficient adaptation
During droughts or food shortages, kangaroos can slow down or delay the development of the young in the pouch.

Devils in danger

Tasmanian devils are solid, large-headed predators found on the Australian island state of Tasmania. These carnivorous little devils are born hunters, using their speed over rough or smooth ground to catch their mostly mammal and bird prey, which their strong jaws and sharp teeth quickly kill. Tough as they are, Tasmanian devils are currently under threat from a fatal face cancer, which has reduced the devil population by 20–50 per cent.

Playing opossum

Opossums range from cat to mouse size and are found in the Americas. Solitary and nomadic they search for carrion and hunt a range of animals including frogs, birds, snakes and other small mammals. Like possums in Australia, they are expert at finding food by rummaging through the garbage in human habitats. If threatened, opossums will often 'play dead', assuming the stiff appearance of a dead animal and giving off a rotten smell to go with the 'dead' look.

The notorious Tasmanian Devil

Migration

Most animal groups contain species that migrate. Some mammals migrate, as do certain fish, reptile, insect and bird species. Birds in particular are famous for making long, and often difficult, dangerous journeys between their summer and winter homes. Animals migrate because of the climate, the availability of food or to breed. Many migrations are a return trip, with the animals travelling in a circular path, while others are a one-way trip.

Wandering Wildebeest

One of the most famous mammal migrations is the annual circular journey undertaken by millions of African Wildebeests. The huge herds travel 2000 kilometres (1200 miles) across the east African savannah, following the fresh grass that the regional rains provide. Thousands of wildebeest die on this long trek, but most survive to make the journey over and over again. Smaller numbers of other antelopes and zebras usually accompany the wildebeest herds.

The annual Wildebeest migration

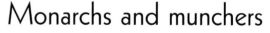
Frequent flyers

Arctic terns migrate each and every year of their adult life. With a 30-year plus lifespan, an Arctic tern can fly over a million kilometres in a lifetime.

Monarchs and munchers

Butterflies and locusts are two insect species that migrate great distances—these frail but fit flutterers can travel thousands of kilometres (miles). Locusts migrate in search of food in vast swarms that can number over 250 million individuals. These can devastate human crops. Butterflies migrate to escape harsh winter weather: American Monarch butterflies have been known to fly over 3000 kilometres (2000 miles) south in their search for the sun. Come spring, the survivors head north again.

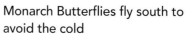
Monarch Butterflies fly south to avoid the cold

A once in a lifetime journey

Salmon make quite a one-way trip back home. As adults, salmon return to the same river where they had been spawned up to eight years earlier. This trip requires them to swim against the current, leap waterfalls and pass other barriers such as bears. Because only the strongest survive the journey it is the fittest individuals who will spawn. It is thought that a strong sense of smell allows salmon to relocate the river where they were born.

Birds on the move

Many birds, including the tiny hummingbird, make massive migrations each year. The furthest flyer record goes to the Arctic tern. After breeding in the Northern Hemisphere summer, the tern leaves the North Pole and heads for the South, travelling up to 20,000 kilometres (125,000 miles) to reach its destination just in time for the South Pole summer. This trip takes about three months and as soon as winter begins down south the terns turn around and make the return trip.

Canada Geese flying in formation

Molluscs

There are about 110,000 species of molluscs—invertebrates with soft, moist bodies and often hard, protective shells. Most molluscs live in water, both salt and fresh, but some species have adapted to a life on the land. There is great variety of shapes, sizes and lifestyles amongst molluscs, ranging from stationary giant clams to swift squid, octopuses and small slow snails.

Slugs and snails

Snail

Snails and slugs make up the largest class of molluscs with around 60,000 species. With so many around, it's not surprising that snails and slugs can be found in nearly all environments. Most are aquatic, but there are also many land living species. Many are herbivores, but there are also carnivores and omnivores, on land and in the sea. Slugs are basically shell-less snails. This leaves them unprotected but able to squeeze into places where snails can't fit.

Blue-ringed Octopus

The octagonal octopus

There are over 300 species of octopus. Despite having three hearts, octopuses don't live for very long—some for as little as six months. They use their eight, often suction-cupped arms to roam the seabed, grabbing a seafood platter of shrimp, crabs, snails and lobsters, which are then shredded in their hard parrot-like beaks. So why have three hearts? Two supply blood for each of the gills, while the third pumps blood around the body.

Giant Clam

Burrowing bivalves

Clams, mussels and oysters are molluscs with a double hinged shell that puts them in the class known as bivalves. Most bivalves are burrowers but some, such as the clams and oysters, spend their lives clinging to rocks and other hard surfaces, anchored on by strong sticky fibres or a form of cement. The biggest bivalve, the giant clam of tropical reefs, can weigh up to 320 kilograms (700 pounds) and span 1.5 metres (5 feet) across.

Stunning shells

Many molluscs use calcium to construct elaborate, often beautifully coloured and patterned shells. These hard protective mobile homes come in many shapes and sizes, though the spiral cone is common. When a marine mollusc dies, its shell often washes up on the shore. Collecting shells is harmless so long as the mollusc is definitely dead. Check by putting it in seawater then watching and waiting—if a mollusc emerges you should leave it alone.

Real-life sea monsters

The biggest mollusc is the rarely encountered giant squid, which reaches a staggering 18 metres (60 feet) in length.

N Navigation

There's a lot we don't know about how animals find their way around, especially on long migrations, or how creatures can pinpoint breeding or spawning grounds, often after years away. Animals use their sense of sight the same way we do, recognising landmarks in their own particular environments. Many use scent trails, or features such as whiskers to help them find their way. When it comes to longer journeys, we are just beginning to learn how big a part the planet might play in assisting animal navigation.

The planet's part

Animals use natural events like the Sun's changing position to assist them in navigating. Bees do on their daily foraging expeditions and birds are likely to also use the Sun to guide migrations of many thousands of kilometres (miles). But researchers are realising that the Earth's magnetic field probably also plays a big part. Sea turtles cross oceans to return to where they were hatched and it is believed that they, along with many other creatures, use the magnetic field as a built-in compass.

Green turtle

Some sort of sense

Many animals use senses like we do, though it is not known how wildebeest and other migrating species of the African savannah know when it is time to be on the move. Do they smell the rain, see the lightning or hear the thunder, so knowing where the rain is falling and fresh green grass will soon be growing? We don't know the answer to these questions, but scientists have observed wildebeests head towards storms hundreds of kilometres (miles) away.

Following their noses

Lost domestic animals such as cats, dogs and horses have all been known to navigate their way tens, hundreds and even thousands of kilometres (miles) back to their homes.

Reading the underwater map

Marine mammals such as toothed whales use sound as a way of finding their way through their underwater world. Echolocation works by sending out high frequency clicking sounds, which are reflected back when they hit an object. Toothed whales use echolocation to avoid underwater obstacles as well as find each other and their prey. For marine mammals without echolocation abilities, the senses of sight and sound are important navigation tools.

Stranded on the sand

Whales beaching themselves is an all-too common occurrence and despite the best efforts of volunteers, many whales die as a result. Why these intelligent animals strand themselves on the shore is not known for sure. However, recent research suggests that it could be linked to interference with the animals' ability to use the Earth's geomagnetic properties when navigating. The causes of this interference might be natural, such as magnetic storms on the Sun's surface, or could be caused by our satellite signals.

Stranded whales on a beach

Nocturnal Animals

Nocturnal animals love the night life and are most active when the Sun is down. Days are spent in burrows, dens or other sunlight-shielding spots. The opposite of nocturnal, used to describe animals that are active during daylight hours, is diurnal. Nocturnal animals have well-developed sight, smell and hearing—cats can see about six times better than humans in darkness—and some such species have extra night-friendly adaptations, such as the echolocation used by bats.

Seeing in the dark

Nocturnal animals need to see well in the dark. Very big eyes with wide pupils and large lenses to collect light are typical—an owl's eyes fill up half its skull size. The eyes of nocturnal animals are structured in a way that greatly reduces sharpness of vision and most are completely colour-blind. But their eyesight is enough to let them see things such as small rodents scurrying about, hoping they are hidden under the cover of darkness.

The real night owls

The 200-odd species of owl are found in all regions except the cold poles and some isolated islands. Most owls hunt small mammals, insects and other birds at dawn, dusk and during darkness. Owls use their keen eyesight to spot prey and their almost silent flight to swoop down quietly but quickly. Like many nocturnal animals, owls cannot move their eyes in their sockets but to compensate for this can rotate their neck 270 degrees.

Southern Boobook Owl

Night vision

Many predators are night hunters, using their strong senses of smell and sight to track their prey under the cover of darkness.

Munching morays

Moray eel

Reefs really come alive at night with many fish and crustaceans emerging after having spent the dangerous day taking cover in cracks, caves and crevices. Some species of moray eel are night feeders, catching fish and crustaceans during darkness. Morays are an oddity—nocturnal hunters with poor night vision. To make up for this, nocturnal eels use their exceptional senses of smell when they slither from their caves and ledges to go hunting.

Why be a night-time animal?

Animals are nocturnal for a number of reasons. Many hot desert dwellers are nocturnal, escaping the heat of the day in some sort of shelter and operating during the cooler night hours, thereby losing much less precious water to evaporation. Some animals are nocturnal for only some of the time—many sea birds and sea turtles come to their colonies and breeding sites only during the night to lessen the likelihood of being targeted by predators.

Thorny Devil

Parasites

Parasites are animals that live on, and feed off another organism. Some live on the outside of their hosts, others burrow into the skin or develop inside. All living organisms play host to at least one parasite, and some have many more. Parasites cause harm to their hosts, ranging from fatigue and sickness to death. Most creatures try to prevent parasites, but a lot of the time they're unstoppable.

Worms within

The longest intestinal parasite pulled out of someone measured over 11 metres (36 feet), while those inside whales can reach over 35 metres (115 feet) in length.

Mosquito sucking blood

Parasites and people

It is estimated that about three-quarters of the world's population play host to intestinal worms. These can cause a heap of problems for people. The deadly killer malaria, passed on by parasitic mosquitoes, kills someone about every 20 minutes. Along with malaria comes a deadly list of diseases including sleeping sickness, river blindness, elephantiasis, Giardia and Ebola, all of which are as bad as they sound.

Itchy and scratchy

Parasites invade either the host's interior or exterior and they are good at it—even parasites can have parasites. Those that survive and thrive inside their hosts are known as endoparasites, such as hookworms, while those that live on or just under the surface like mites are known as ectoparasites. Parasites jump, crawl, get swallowed in food or water, lay eggs or use some other animal for a ride each time they need to change host.

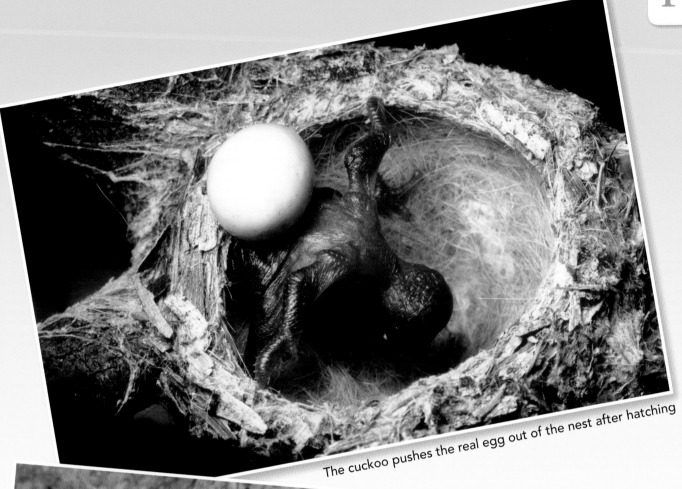

The cuckoo pushes the real egg out of the nest after hatching

Wasps often lay their eggs in other insects, which are then eaten by the wasp larvae when hatched

The clever, cunning cuckoo

Cuckoos are infamous for letting other birds do their egg incubating and chick raising for them, though only about half the 140 species take this parasitic approach to parenting. Cuckoos lay early hatching eggs in a host bird's nest. Building on this head start, young cuckoos grow quickly and soon push the eggs or weaker hatchlings of the host species from the nest. Laying eggs that look like those of the host also helps cuckoos get away with their deceptive behaviour.

Unwelcome dinner guests

Parasitic wasps come into the world with a violent birth. Adults attack, overpower and then lay their eggs inside spiders, caterpillars, moths and many other adult insects or their larvae. The eggs hatch into inside-out parasites, eating the host but leaving the most vital of the unwilling donor's organs until last. Over the time it takes to slowly kill their host, they have formed into adults.

Parrots

There are about 350 species of parrots and cockatoos. Known for their very vocal nature and the vivid colours of their feathers as they flash through the sky, parrots are found in the world's warmer spots, being especially widespread and common in Australasia and South America. They all have short, blunt bills that they use to crack open the seeds, nuts, buds and fruits that form the bulk of their diet. Parrots are very social animals and group together in large and often noisy flocks.

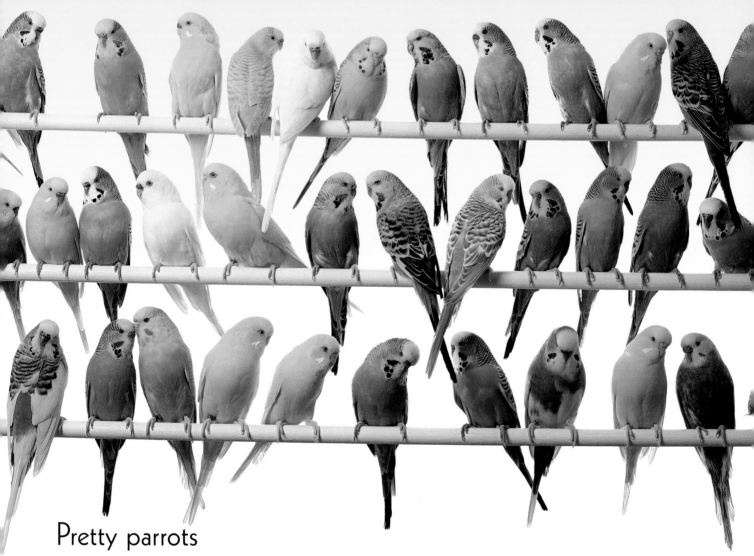

Pretty parrots

Most parrot species have brilliantly coloured and patterned feathers, often green with sprays and splashes of red, yellow, orange, purple and blue. Parrots vary in size and shape, but all have clawed feet with two toes pointing forward and two that point back. A parrot's claws are a top tool for grasping and handling objects. Some parrot species are highly migratory, while others stick to one spot, but most fall somewhere in between when it comes to moving around.

Galahs often nibble clay to keep healthy

Predator parrots

Many parrot species specialise when it comes to food—some are mainly pollen and nectar eaters, while others will kill prey ranging from grubs and water snails to the other birds taken by species such as New Zealand's keas. Other species invade burrows to kill incubating birds. Because the seeds of many plants contain toxins parrots carefully clean away the 'bad bits'. Some species also eat clay, which helps to absorb any plant toxins and provides the parrots with minerals.

Parrot cities

One parrot from northern Argentina lives in deep burrows that the flock digs in cliffs and along river banks.

Sounds smart

For centuries birds have been thought to be not very bright. But that idea is being overturned as experiments on a range of feathered species suggest the opposite—birds can be quite clever. Parrots are known for mimicking other birds and animals, machinery, and the human voice. And they don't just copy—a nearly 30 year study on an African grey parrot showed it to have the naming and counting skills of a five-year-old child!

Parrots in peril

In some ways the parrot's beautiful colours and entertaining abilities have proven a curse, as they are now among the most endangered of birds, with up to a third of species at risk of extinction. Habitat loss is not helping the parrots, but poaching them for the illegal exotic bird trade is believed to be having as big, if not a bigger, threat. Parrot protectors want Asia and Europe to bring in strict laws to stop this species-threatening activity.

Striking colours of the Rainbow Lorikeet

Penguins

When you think of penguins, you probably don't think of deserts. But penguins that live in the dry Antarctic are strictly speaking aquatic desert dwellers. Though penguins live only in the Southern Hemisphere they are not restricted to its cold waters and can be found as far north as the Galapagos Islands. There are about 20 penguin species and one thing they all have in common is that none can fly, though their flipper-like wings are perfect for propelling them through water.

Penguins are remarkable swimmers and are well camouflaged in the water

Pretty perfect parents

Penguins are social birds, gathering and breeding in large flocks. Most penguin parents take equal responsibly for incubating the eggs and raising the offspring. While one baby-sits, the other heads out to sea to find food for the family, a months-long journey that some never return from. Male Emperor penguins shelter the young between their legs, keeping the less insulated chicks off the lethal ice. When they get older, chicks huddle together in large crèches watched over by a few adult birds.

On land and sea

Penguins are not very agile on land, waddling along and looking kind of comical. Once in the water, however, penguins show their diving and swimming skills. Their wings are used as flippers, powering the streamlined birds through the water with great agility at speeds up to 25 kilometres (15 miles) an hour. The most aquatic of birds, penguins can spend up to 20 minutes underwater at depths reaching 200 metres (656 feet) before they need to come up for air.

Group hug
On especially cold days and nights penguins will huddle together in a group in an effort to keep warm, taking turns to be chilled on the edge then toasted in the centre.

Emperor Penguins in Antarctica

Hail to the Emperor

The Emperor Penguine is the tallest and heaviest of all the penguins, standing over a metre tall and weighing up to 35 kilograms (77 pounds). It is one of the few species that lives permanently in Antarctica, even raising chicks in that harsh, icy environment. Like all other penguins, Emperors have a layer of blubber, and very thick fur-like feathers that trap warm air. These adaptations allow them to spend up to 20 minutes underwater in icy seas and also help them float when on the surface.

Seeing things in black and white

The black and white feathers of most penguin species look striking and have a practical purpose. Penguins have no natural predators on land, but things are different in the deep, where they spend half their lives hunting the fish, squid and other sea life that makes up their diet. Predators such as orcas and leopard seals target swimming penguins, so the white belly makes them harder to see from below while the black back helps prevent attacks from above.

Predators

Predators are animals that hunt, catch, kill and eat other animals in order to survive. Predators range in size from tiny insects to large hunters such as big cats, crocodiles and sharks. There are many types of predators and many ways in which they catch their prey, from a sudden ambush to a long chase covering many kilometres in a life and death race. Creatures such as crocodiles and tigers are known as apex predators because they are at the top of their food chains.

Tough at the top

Life can be difficult even for apex predators. Apex predators are big in size but often small in numbers: there are many more prey animals than there are large predators. Because they are so dependent on their prey, the populations of apex predators can drop to dangerously low levels if something causes a drastic reduction in the populations of their main prey species.

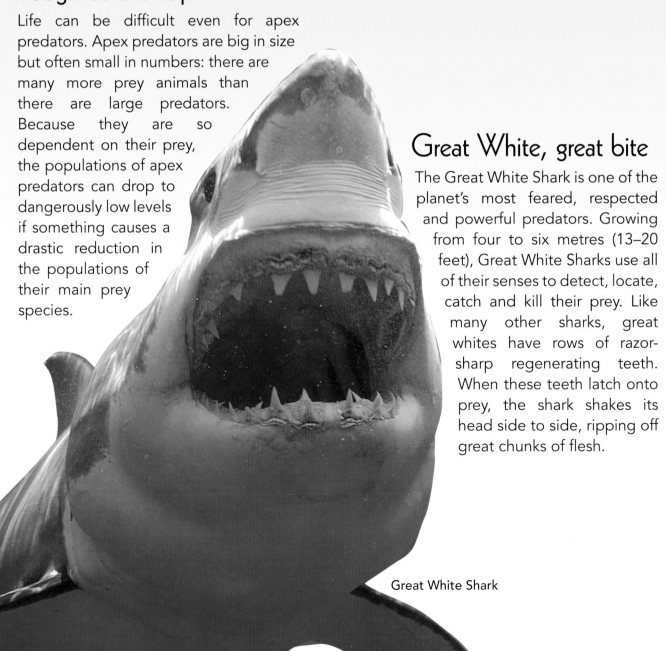

Great White, great bite

The Great White Shark is one of the planet's most feared, respected and powerful predators. Growing from four to six metres (13–20 feet), Great White Sharks use all of their senses to detect, locate, catch and kill their prey. Like many other sharks, great whites have rows of razor-sharp regenerating teeth. When these teeth latch onto prey, the shark shakes its head side to side, ripping off great chunks of flesh.

Great White Shark

Kill or be killed

Unless an animal is an apex predator, life can be a constant battle of wits to survive—as a weasel sneaks up on a frog a snake may be watching both of them while a hawk high above sees all those hunters as potential meals. The concentration required to hunt prey may mean that a predator neglects to keep its senses tuned to anything that may be hunting it, so that the hunter quickly becomes the hunted.

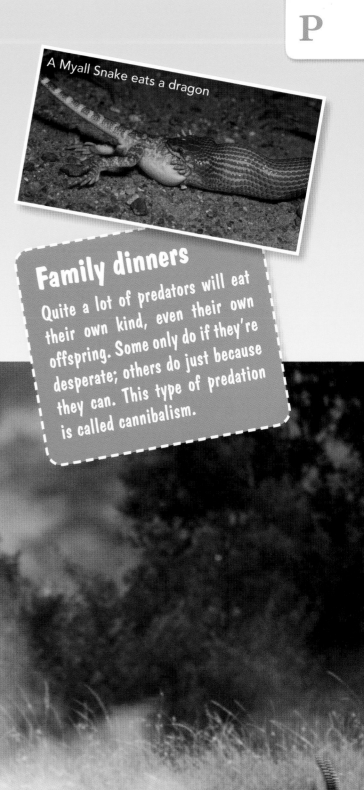

A Myall Snake eats a dragon

Family dinners

Quite a lot of predators will eat their own kind, even their own offspring. Some only do if they're desperate; others do just because they can. This type of predation is called cannibalism.

Born to be wild

Many predators learn the hunting skills they will need in later life by the stalking and pouncing play of their first months. Many parents, particularly mothers, also teach their young basic lessons in hunting. Cheetah mothers will catch but not kill gazelle fawns. The live fawns are brought to the cubs so they can practise the quick killing that will be essential to their survival once they are adults and forced to fend for themselves.

Cheetah hunting down a gazelle

Primates

There are nearly 400 species in the Primate order, including lemurs and monkeys, and apes, which include humans. Primates are found in many environments but tend to favour the warm tropical and subtropical regions. Here many live a largely arboreal life, spending most of their time in the trees. Even mostly ground dwelling species have excellent climbing abilities. Most primates are herbivores or insectivores, though some, such as humans and chimpanzees, will hunt larger prey for meat.

Tooling around

The great apes are known for being clever. Chimpanzees and Orangutans will prepare specially selected sticks to use as tools to obtain termites and other treats. In laboratory research, apes have been taught sign languages of up to 250 words and how to use a variety of objects. They also appear to show self-awareness when they view themselves in a mirror, an ability considered an important indicator of an animal's intelligence.

Going ape

Apes are divided into two main categories—gibbons and the great apes. The great apes grouping includes Asia's orangutans and the African gorillas and chimpanzees. We humans are also part of the ape family. Like humans, the other ape species are very social creatures, living in highly organised groups. Chimpanzee communities can number up to 80 individuals, while gorillas live in smaller family based groups. The mostly solitary orangutan is the main exception to this 'rule'.

Woolley Monkey

Ring-tailed Lemur

Leaping lemurs

Lemurs are found only on the African island of Madagascar, where they have been left to evolve over millions of years. Well adapted to the island's forests, lemurs are mostly nocturnal, feeding on insects along with fruits and flowers. These wide-eyed relatives of the African bushbabies and the lorises of Asia live a wide range of lifestyles—some are solitary or live in pairs, while other species form small, temporary groups or large and permanent communities.

The old and the new

Primates are often divided up into Old World and New World groups. The Old World group contains the monkeys and apes of Africa and Asia, while the latter covers the monkeys of South and Central America. All of the New World monkeys are arboreal and use their strong prehensile tails to move with ease through the trees. None of the Old World monkeys, not even the tree dwellers, have this prehensile tail.

Close cousins

The Chimpanzee is our closest wild relative—we share 99 per cent of our DNA with the Chimps.

R Reptiles

Ancient and armoured, reptiles might look like leftovers from the dinosaur days but they have kept on evolving like most other animals. Reptiles have scales over their dry, thick, waterproof skins and the 8000 plus species have colonised all continents except Antarctica. Unlike birds and mammals, reptiles cannot regulate their internal body temperature. To overcome this, they bask in the sun to warm up and shelter in the shade when they need to cool down.

Not constantly cold blooded

Reptiles are not always truly cold blooded—they only are on cold days. The temperature of a reptile's body rises and falls with the temperature around it. Birds and mammals can regulate their blood's temperature but must use energy to do so; reptiles avoid this energy loss. And while a reptile's temperature can swing up to 30 degrees celsius (86 degrees fahrenheit) without causing it any harm, a few degrees either way from our regular body temperature is enough to kill us.

Ancient giant
The biggest turtle ever was a sea turtle from the late Cretaceous era that was almost five metres long.

Tuatara

Old and unusual

Most reptiles have evolved a lot since their ancestors shared the planet with the dinosaurs. But not New Zealand's tuatara—it has barely changed in 225 million years and its closest relatives haven't been around for 60 million. This has led to the endangered tuatara being labelled a 'living fossil'. Tuataras have not only been around for a long time, they'll be around for many more, continuing to grow for 30 years and living to over 100.

Blood-squirting lizards

When it comes to unusual, it is hard to beat the defensive trick of some horned lizard species. If camouflage, running, burrowing or flattening themselves to the ground doesn't deter a predator, they have one last trick—squirting up to a third of their blood supply from the corners of their eyes! Shooting a distance of over a metre (3 feet), this blood stream startles most predators and also tastes foul. Unfortunately for horned lizards, the only creatures not bothered by the blood are birds—their main predator.

Shapes and sizes

Reptiles come in a range of shapes and sizes. The estuarine crocodiles of northern Australia can grow as long as seven metres, while big pythons can stretch to 10 metres (32 feet). The smallest reptile, a feather-light Caribbean gecko, reaches just 1.6 centimetres (0.6 inches) when fully grown. Most reptiles lay eggs, but a few give birth to live young. Iguanas are an exception to the general meat-eating rule, getting by on fruits, leaves and algae.

Australian estuarine crocodile—an ancient meat-eater

Rodents

Rodents are everywhere with the 2000 species being found across a wide range of habitats and making up nearly half of all the mammal species. Part of the rodent success story stems from their small size and the fact that they reproduce regularly and often, with large litters. The largest living rodent, South America's Capybara, grows to almost 1.3 metres (4.3 feet), dwarfing the less than 50-millimetre-long (2 inches) pygmy jerboa. Squirrels, beavers, prairie dogs, gophers, porcupines and, of course, rats and mice are all rodents.

Mouse gnawing a seed

Eat like a mouse

All rodents have two pairs of front incisor teeth that keep on growing throughout their lifetime. These are self-sharpening and the rodent habit of gnawing at their food helps keep the teeth from growing too long. Most rodents are herbivores and feed on hard plant parts such as seeds, grains and nuts, though a few are predators and some, such as the house mouse, will eat both plants and animals.

Plenty of preying

Most people don't like rats but rodents are extremely popular prey animals—nearly everything wants to eat them! Rodents are on the menus of many bird, reptile and small mammal species. To avoid being eaten, many rodents are nocturnal, while those that are active by day use their strong senses of sight, smell and hearing to try and detect predators before predators find them. Keeping constantly alert and scurrying to the safety of a nearby burrow are other rodent defence strategies.

Busy building beavers

Beavers are the builders of the animal world, constructing dams and canals as well as the lodges where they live. These aquatic rodents have thick oily fur to keep them dry as their flat paddle-like tails and webbed hind feet propel them through the water. Beavers build dams of sticks, branches, stones and mud to ensure they have a calm pond in which to locate their lodge. The lodge is lined with vegetation and provides a warm and dry living area during the long winter months.

The Eurasian Beaver is nature's best builder, constructing dams, canals and lodges

An uneasy relationship

Humans have had a long and often uneasy relationship with rodents, especially some of the mouse and rat species. Many rat and mouse species are opportunistic eaters and this attracts them to human locations such as houses and grain stores. Rats in particular are also feared and disliked because of their role in spreading diseases such as the plague, even though it was the bites from fleas living on the rats that actually caused the often deadly disease.

Lemmings don't leap

Lemmings do not deliberately fling themselves off cliffs, as often believed, but when mass migrations take place panic and the force of numbers can cause many to slip and fall.

Scavengers

Scavengers are animals that feed on the corpses of dead creatures, known as carrion. Hunting often requires the using up of a lot of energy so many predators will take advantage of the easy meal offered up by carrion. Some creatures, such as vultures, feed almost exclusively on what they can scavenge. These scavengers are dependent on the leftovers from large predator kills and the toll taken on other animals by old age, accidents and disease.

Everything has its place

Scavengers such as birds and foxes can often be seen along our roads, feeding on creatures killed by cars. The word 'scavenger' is often used in a negative way, but animal scavengers play an important role in ecosystems by 'cleaning up' the remains of dead creatures. These remains can contain diseases that could spread to healthy animals were they not quickly consumed.

Nature's garbage collectors

Villagers in Africa often put their garbage out for animals such as hyenas to clean up.

Vultures

Though vultures occasionally kill sick or injured animals they mostly let others do the killing for them. Soaring high in the sky, they use their keen eyesight to spot carcasses far below. Once a likely meal is spotted vultures swoop down, crowding around the carcass to fight for the best feeding spots. Many vulture species have 'bald' featherless heads that let them probe deep inside a dead animal's body without getting their feathers all clogged up with gore and guts.

Vultures circle high in the sky until a kill is made, then they swoop to scavenge

Cattle remains

Wolverines

Wolverines are tough, muscular members of the weasel family found in the cold tundra and forests of the Northern Hemisphere. Though strong enough to kill prey much larger than themselves such as moose and reindeer, carrion forms a major part of a wolverine's diet. Surplus food is often buried in tunnels dug under the snow and stored for up to six months for use during lean times.

A hungry army of ants

Found throughout many of the world's tropical regions, army ants clean up the jungle as they migrate in swarms of up to 20 million individuals. Army ants go on the move in search of food, halting to make temporary nests in between migrations. Though they will scavenge whatever food they come across, they will also kill and eat up to 100,000 creatures each day, from bugs to pigs, as they march on.

Sharks

Sharks have been cruising the planet's rivers, seas and oceans for over 400 million years and their relatives, the rays, have been around for about 200 million. During that time they have evolved many adaptations for their watery world. There are over 400 species, ranging in size from the 20 centimetre (8 inches) Spined Pygmy Shark to the largest fish in the sea, the Whale Shark. Sharks and rays differ from other fish in that their skeletons are made up of cartilage, not bone.

Underwater flyers

Close relatives of sharks, rays are known for their distinctive flat, disc-like shape. The broad, flat 'wings' of rays are evolved pectoral fins and are used to propel the rays through the water. The long and slender tails of the rays often have sharp spines that are there to make predators think twice. The flat shape of rays helps these mostly bottom-dwelling fish stay hidden in the sand.

Eagle Rays 'fly' through the sea

Divers swim near a huge Whale Shark

Big fish in big ponds

The largest species of shark are the basking and whale sharks. Both these giants are filter feeders, swallowing huge mouthfuls of water which then passes through their gills, sieving out the tiny plankton they feed on. Basking Sharks are usually found in cooler temperate waters, while the whale shark prefers the warm waters of the tropics. It takes about 25 years for a whale shark to reach maturity and then it still keeps growing, eventually reaching about 15 metres (50 feet) in length.

Our fear of fins

Shark! Just the name is enough to put fear in many people. But it shouldn't—we kill millions of sharks every year, so perhaps they should fear us. There are about 50 reported shark attacks each year, of which about half a dozen are fatal—more people are killed by coconuts. Avoiding swimming at dawn and dusk and not entering the water with open wounds are just two ways you can reduce the already tiny risk of a shark attack.

Shark sense

Sharks use their highly developed senses to locate prey. Good eyesight and an exceptional sense of smell are very important, but it is two other adaptations that help make sharks one of the planet's top predators. Lateral lines running along their bodies help sharks detect movement in the water, such as fish swimming by or a creature struggling. Receptors in the shark's snout, known as Ampullae of Lorenzini, detect the electromagnetic fields produced by all living creatures.

Shark parties

Sharks such as hammerheads sometimes group together in gatherings of hundreds of individuals.

Sloths

Sloths are the slow, sleepy relatives of the anteaters and armadillos. Sloths have a top speed of about 1.5 metres (5 feet) a minute on the ground and though slightly quicker in the trees they spend about 15–18 hours a day asleep. When not resting, sloths feed on leaves and buds and any insects and lizards that come too close. Using their eight to ten-centimetre (3–4 inch) claws to cling to the branches, sloths spend much of their time hanging upside down, even sleeping and giving birth in this position.

Slow-moving sloth

Save the sloth

For such vulnerable animals, sloths have been very successful in their native Central and South America. Though predators such as harpy eagles and jaguars take their toll, the biggest threat facing the sloth is the ongoing destruction of their rainforest habitat. Currently, only one of the six species is classed as 'endangered', but continued habitat loss could see the other sloth species on the 'at-risk' list.

Slow and steady

Nearly everything about the sloth is slow, from their metabolism to their movements. The leaves that make up the bulk of their diet are low in energy and take up to a month to be fully digested. About once a week sloths descend from the trees to pass solid wastes. Unable to support their own body weight they drag themselves to the base of their preferred toilet trees.

Sloths are well hidden in the foliage

Tree huggers

Sloths are at their most vulnerable on the ground, so they spend most of their time in the trees where their slow movements and camouflaged coats help them keep a low profile. But even here they are not 100 per cent safe. Harpy eagles are powerful birds that can snatch an adult sloth from the treetops and carry it back, still alive, to the waiting and hungry eagle chicks.

Green with algae

Sloths have nothing other than claws to defend themselves with, so keeping quiet and moving slowly not to attract attention is a sloth's best bet for staying alive. Some sloth species have long fur that is tinged green by the algae that grows on it. Not only does licking the algae-coated fur provide the sloth with extra nutrients, the colouring also helps it to blend in with the leaves.

Swimming for safety

Sloths are surprisingly good swimmers and move quicker through the water than they can on land.

Snakes and Lizards

With around 4500 species of lizards and almost 3000 different snakes, these are by far the most numerous reptiles. Most have the same streamlined shape—though snakes are legless—but there is much diversity in size, habitats and habits. All snakes and most lizards are meat eaters that use many different methods to get a meal. Many snakes use venom to kill prey, while lizards mostly rely on a sudden pounce and snap. To find prey both rely on their tongues—the organ they use to smell with.

Lookout lizards

Most snakes are too big to be viewed as prey by many predators, and many have venom as extra protection. Lizards look defenceless in comparison, and many do fall prey to a whole range of creatures, especially birds and smaller mammals. But some species have a few tricks. Camouflage is one, helping them to blend into the background. Hissing, raising up frilled necks or sharp spines, and of course running, are all other methods by which lizards avoid each day being their last.

Colourful chameleons and garish geckos

Geckos are among the most dazzling of lizards, with many of the nearly 2000 species displaying brilliant colours and striking patterns. Some geckos can also change the colour of their skin to blend in with their surroundings and all chameleons have this ability. Chameleons can also turn their eyeballs 360 degrees. Geckos too have a unique quality among lizards—they can make a wide variety of barking, clicking and squeaking sounds.

Beware the Gila

Though snakes are known for their venom, only one species of lizard has the ability to kill by poison—the squat Gila monster of the southwest USA.

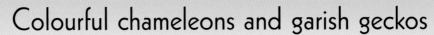

Colourful chameleons are masters of disguise

A Stimsons Python strangling its prey

Bacteria-breathing dragons

Indonesia's Komodo Dragon is the world's longest, heaviest lizard, reaching up to three metres in length and weighing up to 90 kilograms (200 pounds). Mostly slow creatures, Komodo Dragons use their keen sense of smell to locate carrion, but will also hunt a wide range of animals. Their mouths are full of fast-acting bacteria which can quickly kill prey that, having been bitten, escape the initial ambush. The dragons simply follow the trail of blood until they catch up with the weakened prey.

Komodo Dragons are the world's largest lizards

Venomous strikers and killer constrictors

Venom is a liquid that contains paralysing and often deadly toxins. Venomous snakes kill or immobilise their prey with this lethal injection. Constrictors used a different method—after seizing their prey they coil themselves tightly round it. By keeping the pressure on, constrictors prevent the prey from breathing, leading to death by suffocation, not crushing as often thought. The dead prey of both venomous and constrictor species is usually swallowed whole and can take days or even weeks to digest.

Turtles and Tortoises

Having been around since before the dinosaurs, turtles and tortoises have had plenty of time to evolve and find their niche. The main difference between them is that tortoises live on land and have broad, clawed feet, while turtles are aquatic with webbed feet or flippers. The only reptiles with a shell, there are nearly 300 species ranging from the 900 kilogram (2000 pound) Leatherback Sea Turtle to a South African tortoise that is eight centimetres long and weighs 140 grams (5 oz). Their diets vary—some are predators, others rely on plant matter or scavenging for their nutritional needs.

The giant Galapagos Tortoise

Slow and steady

While turtles can swim with ease underwater, tortoises on land are not known for their fast pace—a migrating bog turtle can take two weeks to cover a distance of 180 metres (600 feet).

Turtle hatchlings start their perilous journey to the sea

A scramble to the surf

Sea turtles return to the same beaches, year after year, to lay their eggs in a sand-covered nest and then leave. When the young turtles hatch they must run a gauntlet of waiting predators to reach the slightly safer sea. Once they enter the water they are still in peril from fish and other marine predators, but at least they've survived the dangerous, often deadly, scramble across the sand. In some species only about one in 50,000 hatchlings will reach maturity.

Webbed feet are perfect for swimming

Turtles in trouble

With over 25 species listed as critically endangered and nearly 50 classed as endangered, turtles and tortoises are in a bit of bother. Habitat loss, being hunted for food and traditional medicines and capture for the pet trade are all impacting on turtle and tortoise numbers, which have shown a sudden decline over the last decade. The turtle's shell protects it from most predators but can do nothing to save those species that are under attack from human activity.

Shell Shock

Both turtles and tortoises have strong protective shells that cover the tops and bottoms of their bodies, a feature that makes them unique among reptiles. The shell is actually an extension of the animal's ribs and backbone, meaning that they are stuck with it for life. Shell shapes and sizes vary depending on the animal's habitat and lifestyle but all use them as a deterrent and defence against predators, pulling their soft parts back inside whenever danger threatens.

Fresh or Salty?

Some turtle species are freshwater dwellers, while others live a more marine life. Freshwater turtles have long legs with webbed feet and claws. Found in creeks, rivers and lakes, many species hibernate during the colder months as, being cold blooded, they cannot regulate their body temperature. Sea turtles are found throughout the world's warmer waters where they use their forelimb flippers to swim through the sea, rarely emerging except to nest.

Venomous Animals

Venomous animals are those that use venom, a toxic solution, to defend themselves or kill their prey. Snakes and spiders are among the best known venomous animals but many other creatures have venom at their disposal, including some insects, jellyfish and corals and even some mammals. Venom is delivered in a range of ways including by biting or stinging or by using tentacles or a structure known as a proboscis. Most venom kills the prey swiftly so it cannot escape the hungry predator.

What's your poison?

Different types of venom work in different ways, but all are painful and bad news for the bitten. Neurotoxins attack the nervous system and can lead to lung failure and heart attack, while hemotoxins affect the circulatory system. Venoms that are hemotoxic are particularly painful and the effects include stopping the blood from clotting and major tissue damage. Hemotoxins also help predators digest their prey.

Snake being milked for its venom

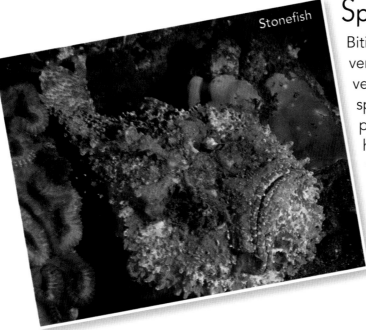

Stonefish

Special delivery

Biting and stinging are typical ways in which venom is injected but there are many other venom variations. Stonefish use 13 hollow spines for delivering their extremely powerful, painful venom; stingrays have a hard serrated spine near the base of their tail. Jellyfish have stinging cells on their tentacles, which are used to paralyse prey; creatures such as cone shells use a venom-filled dart attached to their proboscis. Some snakes even spit venom as a warning rather than to catch or kill.

A jellyfish with stinging tentacles trailing

Toxic terms

Poisonous is not the same as venomous—venoms are injected while poisons are absorbed through the skin or when a poisonous creature, such as a puffer fish, is eaten.

Saving for dinnertime

Venomous creatures rely on their stockpile of poison for both defence and attack. Venom takes time to replenish itself so most animals wisely choose when to use it and how much to inject. When snakes bite something in order to deter it, they often inject no venom in what is called a 'dry bite'. They do this because the snake sees the intruder as a threat, not a feed, and chooses to save its venom for mealtimes.

Deadliest of the deadly bunch

It is difficult to determine exactly which venomous animals are the deadliest but there are a few that will be found on all the top ten lists. Snakes are widely known as venomous but the majority of snake species are not. Of those that are, the Australian taipan has very potent venom, along with that of the sea snakes. When it comes to stingers, species such as the box jellyfish have particularly potent venom.

W Whales and Dolphins

Whales and dolphins come under the order of Cetaceans, mammals which have adapted to an almost totally aquatic life and need only to emerge to breathe. Cetaceans can be divided into two groups—toothed and baleen whales. Baleens are the biggest, and have plates instead of teeth that are used for straining tiny creatures such as krill or small fish from the water. As the name suggests, toothed whales such as Orcas and dolphins use their sharp teeth to grasp prey such as fish and crustaceans, which are then usually swallowed whole.

Tusks and teeth

The Narwhal is a dweller of the icy Arctic waters with an unusual adaptation. Male narwhals have a large spiral tusk projecting from their upper jaw, which can grow to lengths of nearly three metres. We know that the tusk is an extended incisor tooth, but aren't sure what its purpose is. Once thought to be an ice-breaking tool, the most recent thinking is that the tusk might be a sensory device, supplying the Narwhal with information on the surrounding water conditions.

Mythical creatures

Sightings of narwhals by early sailors and the bringing back of their tusks to Europe are believed to have played a part in beliefs about the mythical unicorn.

A Narwhal comes to the surface to breathe

The big blue

The largest creature on the planet, in fact the largest that has ever lived, is the massive Blue Whale. Blue Whales are able to grow to lengths of 33 metres (108 feet) and reach a weight of 180 tonnes (that's about 35 elephants!) because the watery environment supports their huge bulk. The Blue Whale has no natural predators, other than packs of orcas, but widespread hunting throughout much of the 20th century has seen even this gentle giant ending up on the endangered list.

Aquatic adaptations

Like all mammals, cetaceans are warm-blooded, breathe air into their lungs and feed their young milk. Then things start to differ—the cetaceans have streamlined bodies, like those of fish. This, combined with their paddle-shaped forelimbs and powerful tails, allows them to move smoothly through the water. When it comes time to take a breath—and some cetaceans can stay underwater for up to two hours—they use blowholes situated on the top of their heads.

Wolves of the sea

The distinctive black and white Orcas, or Killer Whales, are also sometimes called the 'wolves of the sea' because they are very successful at pack hunting large prey. Even very big animals such as other whales can fall victim to a pack of Orcas. Even being on land is no guarantee of safety—Orcas are known for coming up onto beaches to snatch a seal from the sand, then waiting for the next wave to take them both back out to sea.

An Orca stalks seals on the shore

Wolves

These wild relatives of the domestic dog are found across much of the Northern Hemisphere and parts of northern Africa. There are three species of wolf—the Grey, the Red and the rare Ethiopian Wolf, which may in fact be a jackal! There is a lot of variety within wolf species, with the Grey Wolf having up to a dozen sub-species. The size, colour and lifestyle of wolves are all affected by their environment, but the home ranges of many of the sub-species often overlap.

A howling shame

With only about 500 left in the wild, Africa's Ethiopian Wolf is one of the planet's most endangered animals.

Wolf talk

Sound and sight are two of the ways wolves make their mood known to other wolves. Growls, howls, barks and whimpers form part of a wolf's 'language'. Growls and barks are usually used as a warning, while howling is used for long distance communication between pack members. Whimpering during disputes is a wolf's way of saying 'I give up, you win'. Body language and a wide range of facial expressions further add to a wolf's ways of expressing itself.

A wolf howling

Running with the pack

Wolves are social animals and most live in packs. At the top of a pack is a male and female pair, usually the oldest, most experienced individuals. The other wolves follow this top pair in hunting and travelling decisions. Pack size varies, but the larger Grey wolf tends to live in packs of up to a dozen, while Red wolves live in slightly smaller groups. Pack life allows for cooperation in hunting, protection for pups and the company of other wolves.

Villains or victims?

For thousands of years people have believed wolves were very dangerous. And to many animals, both wild and domestic, they can be, but wolves pose little threat to us and there are very few verified attacks on humans. Given that humans have been shooting, trapping and poisoning wolves for centuries, they have much more reason to fear us than we have to be scared of them.

Wolves are pack animals that hunt and travel together

Return to the wild

Wolves have been driven out of many of their environments—especially when their home range overlaps with humans and our domesticated animals—but in recent years wolf packs have been reintroduced to places such as Yellowstone National Park, where for centuries they had roamed free. Some people have opposed these moves but the wolves themselves are thriving, and their presence helps prevent overpopulation in their main prey species of deer and other large mammals.

Zebras

Zebras, with their stunning black and white designs, are ungulates that are found in a range of African environments. There are three species of zebra—the widespread and numerous Plains zebra and the endangered Grevy's and Mountain zebras. As prey animals, zebras need to stay alert to stay alive. Large ears and good eyesight, quick reflexes and a fast turn of speed, plus the protection of the herd, are all tactics used by zebras to try and out-sense and outrun predators.

On the trot

As easy prey animals in an environment full of predators, zebra foals have to be up and about very soon after being born. Within 20 minutes of birth a foal is able to walk and by the time an hour has gone by they are up and running. Zebras keep on the move in search of water and food, and both mother and foal need to keep up with the herd for safety.

Herds and harems

A herd of zebras moving across the plains looks like one huge group, but this mass of mammals is actually made up of smaller family units, called harems. Each harem consists of a stallion, about half a dozen mares, and their foals. Each stallion keeps his family group together and chases off other males. Males without a harem live alone or in small groups, waiting for an opportunity to take over another stallion's family.

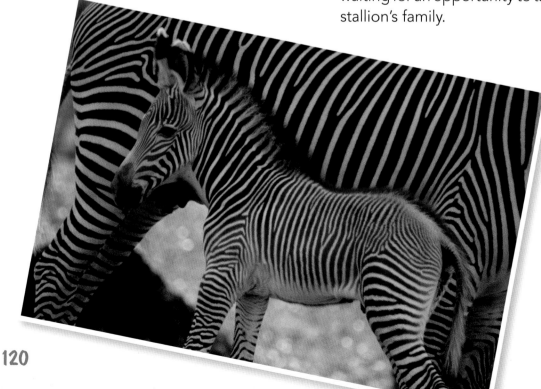

Zebra talk

Zebras are social animals with a range of ways of communicating. Facial expressions and the position of the ears alert other zebras to an individual's mood. Upright ears usually indicate a calm zebra, while ears forward can mean a frightened individual and ears back signals an angry zebra. A range of calls that includes whinnying, snorting and barking add to the zebra 'language' while mutual grooming strengthens the bonds between the members of a herd.

What's with the stripes?

A zebra's stripes, like a human's fingerprints, are unique. This helps zebras recognise individuals, including mothers and their foals. When zebras move through long grass the vertical stripes help them blend in and though the black and white stripes stand out to us, lions are colour-blind. For further protection, when a herd of zebras are fleeing the stripes help make them look like one large mass, making it more difficult for predators to isolate an individual.

Activities

25 QUICK QUESTIONS

1. What animal is also known as a gnu?

2. Only one type of bear is found on the South American continent—what is it called?

3. Why do firefly larvae produce light?

4. What animals regularly make use of thermal currents and why?

5. What produces the patterns on a butterfly's wings?

6. What animals are collectively called 'pinnipeds'?

7. What is the only living thing that can be seen from space?

8. How many species of crustaceans are there roughly—5000, 50,000 or 500,000?

9. What animal spends up to 20 hours a day finding the 150 kilograms (330 pounds) of food it will consume?

10. True or false—there are more tigers found in zoos than there are living in the wild?

11. What are brumbies and mustangs?

12. Hyenas live in matriarchal groups—what does this mean?

13. How many stomachs does a starfish have?

14. About how many species of mammal are there—425, 4250 or 42,500?

15. What is the biggest threat currently facing Tasmanian Devils?

16. How many hearts does an octopus have?

17. Certain species of a type of bird lays its eggs in the nests of other birds. What are these nest robbers known as?

18. What bird can spend up to 20 minutes underwater?

19. Eating others members of the same species as yourself is known as?

20. Which New Zealand reptile has barely changed for the past 225 million years?

21. A swarm of army ants can number 200,000, 20 million or 200 million individual ants?

22. Which jungle-dwelling mammal can often be seen with green algae growing on its fur?

23. About how many baby turtles will survive out of every 50,000 hatched—1, 10 or 1000?

24. Which type of venom prevents blood from clotting—neurotoxins or hemotoxins?

25. How long does it usually take a newborn zebra foal to be able to run with the herd— 10 minutes, one hour or one day?

ANSWERS ARE ON PAGE 128

Activities

MATCH THE MEANINGS

See if you can match the words below to what they mean about animals and their lifestyles.

ARBOREAL   HABITAT   TERRESTRIAL   PREDATOR

PARASITISM   AQUATIC   MARINE   HIBERNATE

ECOSYSTEM   DIURNAL   NOCTURNAL   CAMOUFLAGE

· Lives all or most of the time in the seas or oceans
· Most active at night time
· Most active during daylight hours
· Spends most of the colder months in an inactive state
· Patterns, colours and body shapes that allow an animal to blend in against the background
· Lives all or most of the time on land
· Lives by hunting, killing and eating other animals

· The particular area within an environment in which an animal lives
· Where a plant or animal lives off another plant or animal
· Lives all or most of the time in trees
· The plants, animals and other natural features in an area
· Lives all or most of the time in the water

IT'S ALL IN THE NAME

The scientific and local names for many animals often come from the creature's habits and habitats, appearance and actions. See if you can match the descriptions below with the animals they are talking about.

1. This class is named for the Latin term for 'to creep'.

2. These animals are named after the Latin term for 'flesh devourers'.

3. One Spanish name for this South American resident means 'bull killer'.

4. The Latin name for this order of mammals means 'to gnaw'

5. This animal's name comes from two Greek words—one meaning 'horn' and the other 'nose'.

6. The order of these insects, Lepidoptera, means 'scale wing' in Greek.

7. This group gets its name from the crusty exoskeleton all the members have.

8. The Latin name for these predators means 'to seize and carry away'.

9. The Greek word for this animal means 'water horse'.

10. The Latin name for the order of these amphibians means 'lacking tail'.

11. The Latin name for these creatures means 'pouched mammals'.

12. The name for this order of animals means 'hand wing'.

ANSWERS ARE ON PAGE 128

More Activities

WHAT AM I?

Try working backwards to see how quickly you can narrow the clues down to the animal they refer to.

1. I am a large ungulate.
   There are two species of me, both found on the African savannah.
   One species is the 'black' and the other is the 'blue'.
   Mostly I live in large herds for protection from predators.
   Each year many of me go on a long, exhausting and dangerous migration.

2. I'm an invertebrate with a soft moist body.
   I am part of the most numerous group within my phylum.
   I differ from my closest relative by having a hard, protective and often colourful shell.
   I am a type of mollusc.
   My closest relatives are the slugs.

3. I am a vertebrate that hatches from an egg.
   I am related to birds but I'm not one.
   I use the sun to help regulate my body temperature.
   I spend much of my time in water.
   I prey on both terrestrial and aquatic animals.
   My jaw is V shaped unlike my closest relative's.

4. I'm part of a group that's been on Earth for a long time.
   I was one of the first of this group to move from the water to the land.
   I am an opposite of invertebrate.
   I have four legs and a tail.
   I always live in moist places.
   I'm an often brightly coloured amphibian.
   I use my tongue to catch prey.

5. I'm an aerial animal.
   Some other animals find me useful.
   I find food by looking for signs of life and death while floating high on thermals.
   Nearly all this food is scavenged.
   I'm a raptor with an often bald head.

ANSWERS ARE ON PAGE 128

Glossary

ARTHROPODS animals with jointed legs and hard exoskeletons such as insects, arachnids and crustaceans.

BACTERIA microscopic single-celled organisms

CALCIUM mineral that the body uses to maintain the health of teeth and bones

CAMOUFLAGE patterns, colours and body shapes that allow an animal to blend in against the background

CAPTIVITY animals, both domestic and wild, that are kept and cared for by humans

CARTILAGE connecting tissue that provides structure and support such as in the human nose

COCOON a protective silk case made by some insects and spiders

CRÈCHES groups of young animals looked after and over by adult members of the species

DESERTS areas that receive little rain or snow fall

DORMANT describes the time when an animal is engaging in no activity

DUNG an animal's droppings

ENZYMES molecules that speed up a chemical reaction

ESTUARIES partly enclosed coastal bodies of water that are fed by both tides and rivers and streams flowing in

EXOSKELETON a hard external skeleton

FOOD WEB the relationships between all the species in an ecosystem in terms of what eats what

FRY young fish

GESTATION PERIOD the length of an animal's pregnancy

HATCHLINGS young birds or reptiles that have just emerged from the egg

HIBERNATE to spend most of the colder months in an inactive state

LARVAE young creatures that look and often act different from the adult specimens they will eventually become via complete metamorphosis

MATURITY when an animal is old enough to breed

MEMBRANE a thin, soft, flexible layer of tissue

METABOLISM the chemical reactions that allow an organism to survive

NICHE the role played by a species within its community

NUTRIENTS essential substances that an animal obtains from the food it eats

NYMPH the young stage of insects that do not undergo complete metamorphosis

OMNIVOROUS animals that eat both plants and other animals

PRAIRIES the grasslands of North America

PREHENSILE an organ that is used for grasping and gripping

PROBOSCIS in insects, a tube-shaped mouth part that is used for obtaining food

PUPA the stage at which an insect develops from larvae into a fully grown state

RABIES a deadly viral disease that causes inflammation of the brain

REGURGITATED to throw up or pour from a cavity

SAVANNAH grasslands with scattered trees and shrubs

SECRETE to produce and discharge a substance from cells or body fluids

SINEWS tough tissues connecting muscles to bone

SPAWN to deposit large numbers of eggs into the water

SUBTERRANEAN anything that is or lives underground

TOXIC a chemical or other substance that is poisonous and causes damage to living organisms

TUNDRA cold regions where the soil is often frozen and only small plants grow

UNGULATE mammals that have hooves and eat plants

UNIQUE being the only one of its kind

WEANED animals that no longer rely on their mother's milk for nutrients

Want to Know More?

If you want to know more about the animals is this book or the many many others that are out there in our wide and sometimes wild world, the websites below might be a good place to start. Some sites are about zoos, others are about conservation and how you can help wildlife locally or around the world, while others just have oodles of interesting info on animals.

A WEB FULL OF ANIMALS

www.zoo.org.au
www.currumbin-sanctuary.org.au
www.perthzoo.wa.gov.au/index.html
www.zoo.nsw.gov.au
www.reptilepark.com.au
www.wmi.com.au/crocpark
http://seaworld.myfun.com.au/
www.sydneyaquarium.com.au
www.worldwildlife.org
www.wilderness.org.au
www.greenpeace.org.au
www.wwf.org
www.hsi.org.au
www.blueplanetbiomes.org
www.allaboutanimals.org.uk
www.kids.nationalgeographic.com
www.australianfauna.com
www.abc.net.au/schoolstv/animals/default.htm
www.kidcyber.com.au/topics/animals.htm
www.kidzone.ws

Latin Names

AARDWOLF (*Proteles cristatus*)

AFRICAN ELEPHANT (*Loxodonta africana*)

AFRICAN GOLIATH FROG (*Conraua goliath*)

AFRICAN LION (*Panthera leo*) + JAGUAR (*Panthera onca*)

AFRICAN WILD DOGS (*Lycaon pictus*)

AMERICAN ALLIGATOR (*Alligator mississippiensis*)

AMERICAN BISON (*Bison bison*)

AMERICAN BLACK BEAR (*Ursus americanus*)

AMERICAN LOBSTER (*Homarus americanus*)

AMERICAN MONARCH BUTTERFLY (*Danaus plexippus*)

ANTILOPINE KANGAROO (*Macropus antilopinus*)

ARCTIC TERN (*Sterna paradisaea*)

ASIAN ELEPHANT (*Elephas maximus*)

BASKING SHARK (*Cetorhinus maximus*)

BLUE WHALE (*Balaenoptera musculus*)

BROWN HYENA (*Hyaena brunnea*)

BUMBLEBEE BAT (*Craseonycteris thonglongyai*)

CANE TOAD (*Bufo marinus*)

CAPYBARA (*Hydrochoerus hydrochaeris*)

CHINESE ALLIGATOR (*Alligator sinensis*)

COYOTE (*Canis latrans*)

CROWN-OF-THORNS STARFISH (*Acanthaster planci*)

DEATH WATCH BEETLE (*Xestobium rufovillosum*)

DINGO (*Canis lupus dingo*)

DOMESTIC DOG (*Canis lupus familiaris*)

DUGONG (*Dugong dugon*)

EASTERN GREY KANGAROO (*Macropus giganteus*)

EMPEROR PENGUIN (*Aptenodytes forsteri*)

ETHIOPIAN WOLF (*Canis simensis*)

EUROPEAN BISON (*Bison bonasus*)

GIANT CLAM (*Tridacna gigas*)

GIANT ELAND (*Taurotragus derbianus*)

GIANT PANDA (*Ailuropoda melanoleuca*)

GILA MONSTER (*Heloderma suspectum*)

GOLDFISH (*Carassius auratus*)

GOLIATH BIRD-EATING SPIDER (*Theraphosa blondi*)

GREAT WHITE SHARK (*Carcharodon carcharias*)

GREVY'S ZEBRA (*Equus grevyi*)

GREY WOLF (*Canis lupus*)

HARVESTER BUTTERFLY (*Feniseca tarquinius*)

HIPPOPOTAMUS (*Hippotomus amphibius*)

JAPANESE SPIDER CRAB (*Macrocheira kaempferi*)

JAVA FLYING FROG (*Rhacophirus reinwardtii*)

KODKOD (*Leopardus guigna*)

KOMODO DRAGON (*Varanus komodoensis*)

LEATHERBACK SEA TURTLE (*Dermochelys coriacea*)

MEERKAT (*Suricata suricatta*)

MOUNTAIN ZEBRA (*Equus zebra zebra*)

NARWHAL (*Mondon monoceros*)

ORCA (*Orcinus orca*)

PASSENGER PIGEON (*Ectopistes migratorius*)

PEREGRINE FALCON (*Falco peregrinus*)

PLAINS ZEBRA (*Equus quagga*)

POLAR BEAR (*Ursus maritimus*)

POTATO BEETLE (*Lema trilineata*)

PYGMY HIPPO (*Hexaprotodon liberiensis*)

RED KANGAROO (*Macropus rufus*)

RED WOLF (*Canis rufus*)

ROYAL ANTELOPE (*Neotragus pygmaeus*)

SAIGA ANTELOPE (*Saiga tatarica*)

SEA OTTER (*Enhydra lutris*)

SLOTH BEAR (*Melursus ursinus*)

SNAIL KITE (*Rostrhamus sociabilis*)

SNOW LEOPARD (*Uncia uncia*)

SPECTACLED BEAR (*Tremarctos ornatus*)

SPOTTED HYENA (*Crocuta crocuta*)

STRIPED HYENA (*Hyaena hyaena*)

TASMANIAN DEVIL (*Sarcophilus harrisii*)

THYLACINE (*Thylacinus cynocephalus*)

TIGER (*Panthera tigris*) + LEOPARD (*Panthera pardus*)

WALRUS (*Odobenus rosmarus*)

WATERBUCK (*Kobus ellipsiprymnus*)

WEDGE-TAILED EAGLE (*Aquila audax*)

WESTERN GREY KANGAROO (*Macropus fuliginosis*)

WESTERN HONEY BEE (*Apis mellifera*)

WHALE SHARK (*Rhincodon typus*)

WOLVERINE (*Gulo gulo*)

Answers

25 QUICK QUESTIONS

1. Wildebeest 10–11
2. Spectacled bear 16–17
3. So predators know they contain chemicals that make them bad to eat 20–21
4. Birds; use them to stay aloft without using energy to beat their wings 24–25
5. Overlapping scales of different colours 30–31
6. Seals, sea lions and walruses 34–35
7. Australia's Great Barrier Reef 38–39
8. About 50,000 42–43
9. Elephant 48–49
10. True 50–51
11. Feral horses found in Australia and the USA 56–57
12. That the leaders of the group are female 66–67
13. Two 70–71
14. About 4250 76–77
15. Facial cancer with almost 100% mortality rate 80–81
16. Three 84–85
17. Cuckoos 90–91
18. Penguin 94–95
19. Cannibalism 96–97
20. Tuatara 100–101
21. 20 million 104–105
22. Sloths 108–109
23. One 112–113
24. Hemotoxins 114–115
25. One hour 120–121

MATCH THE MEANINGS

ARBOREAL — Lives all or most of the time in trees

PARASITISM — Where a plant or animal lives off another plant or animal

ECOSYSTEM — The plants, animals and other natural features in an area

HABITAT — The particular area within an environment in which an animal lives

AQUATIC — Lives all or most of the time in the water

DIURNAL — Most active during daylight hours)

TERRESTRIAL — Lives all or most of the time on land

MARINE — Lives all or most of the time in the seas or oceans

NOCTURNAL — Most active at night time

PREDATOR — Lives by hunting, killing and eating other animals

HIBERNATE — Spends most of the colder months in an inactive state

CAMOUFLAGE — Patterns, colours and body shapes that allow an animal to blend in against the background

IT'S ALL IN THE NAME

1. Reptilia
2. Carnivore
3. Anaconda
4. Rodentia/rodents
5. Rhinoceros
6. Butterflies and moths
7. Crustaceans
8. Raptors/birds of prey
9. Hippopotamus
10. Frogs and toads
11. Marsupials
12. Bats

WHAT AM I?

1. Wildebeest
2. Snail
3. Crocodile
4. Salamander
5. Vulture

£8.99